Everlasting Life Reminder

By Brenda Genaro

Authentic Works Publishing
Anchorage, Alaska

EVERLASTING LIFE REMINDER

Authentic Works Publishing
Anchorage, Alaska 99508

ISBN 978-0-578-91242-4

The Bible passages used in this book are from the New King James Version of the Bible unless otherwise stated.

Photographs by Brenda Genaro

Words of the Song "We'll Understand It Better By And By" by Charles Albert Tindley, 1851-1933 Arr. by F.A. Clark

Journal Entry "My Philosophy of Life" written by Richard Alan Genaro.

Journal Entry "Why Fathers are Proud of Their New Born Babies" written by Richard Alan Genaro.

"When Grief is Finished," excerpt from Odyssey Health Care Hospice of Alabama. Written by Chaplain Jim Metzler and Chaplain Craig Greer.

Manufactured in the United States of America
First printing May 2021

Dedication

To My Father and Mother, Husband, and Children.

Acknowledgement

With appreciation to Editor Rob Bignell, whose professionalism, literary excellence, and straightforward approach to writing and editing, contributed greatly to the completion of this book.

Contents

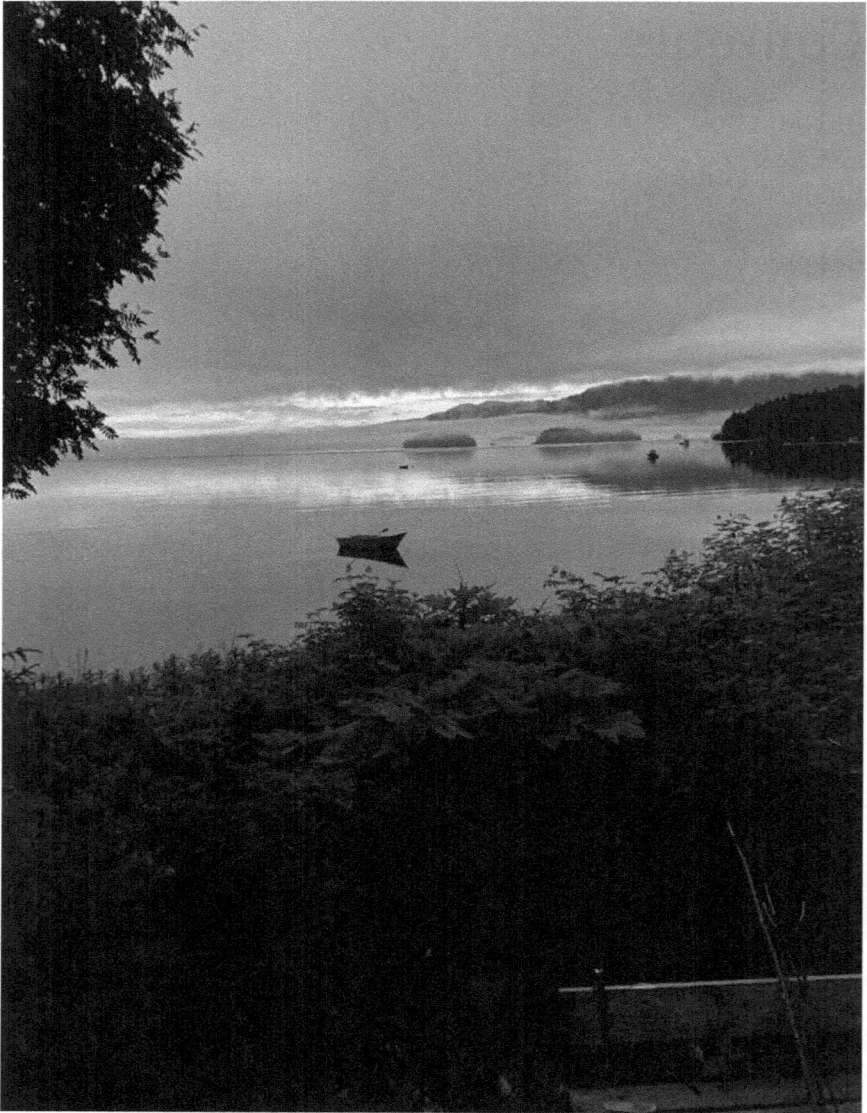

Introduction

Grieving

The seasons grieving for a loved one who has passed away may be some of the darkest seasons of your life. There aren't any words that can be said to take away the pain. If I could change what happened, I would. Yet, I can't.

Take a deep breath.

Inhale slowly...

Exhale slowly...

and breathe.

In your grief, your excruciating pain, remember to breathe.

The true love you shared with your loved one, survived physical death, and will last forever. You will be with your loved ones again in everlasting life. Sometimes, through the tears, these words can be a gentle reminder of salvation you have in Christ.

And this is the promise that He has promised us – eternal life. 1 John 2:25

Remember to Breathe

Please be gentle and kind to yourself. Experiencing shock of sudden trauma can have unexpected effects on the human mind and body. With this realization, it is important to take care of yourself. Especially, as you are trying to understand what's happened.

***

Thinking of everlasting life may be difficult, as you miss your loved one. Life as you knew it has changed. Know that you can live with a broken heart. Live through the pain toward healing. You can breathe, even though it seems like you aren't able to take another breath. You can breathe.

And the Lord God formed man of the dust of the ground, and breathed into his nostrils the breath of life; and man became a living being. Genesis 2:7

The Spirit of God has made me, and the breath of the Almighty gives me life. Job 33:4

The answers to your questions will be revealed when the time is right for you. The words of a song by Charles Albert Tindley (Arr. by F.A. Clark), says it all. Instead of singing, carefully read the chorus and stanza or verse 3 and 4 and let the words enter your mind...

We'll Understand It Better By and By

By and by, when the morning comes,
All the saints of God are gathered home,
We'll tell the story how we've overcome,
For we'll understand it better by and by
Trials dark on ev'ry hand,
And we cannot understand
All the ways that God would lead us
To that blessed promised land;
But he guides us with his eye,
And we'll follow till we die,
For we'll understand it better by and by
By and by, when the morning comes,
All the saints of God are gathered home,
We'll tell the story how we've overcome,
For we'll understand it better by and by
Temptations, hidden snares
Often take us unawares,
And our hearts are made to bleed
For a thoughtless word or deed,
And we wonder why the test
When we try to do our best,
But we'll understand it better by and by.
By and by, when the morning comes,
All the saints of God are gathered home,
We'll tell the story how we've overcome,
For we'll understand it better by and by

Living Scriptures

The Lord is my Shepherd; I shall not want. He makes me to lie down in green pastures; He leads me beside the still waters. He restores my soul; He leads me in the paths of righteousness For His name's sake. Yea, though I walk through the valley of the shadow of death I will fear no evil; For You are with me; Your rod and Your staff, they comfort me. Psalm 23:1-4

The Light of the Lord will illuminate your way. His Holy Spirit has been with you and in you through all the seasons of your life. He is still with you in this season of grief. Even if the trauma and heaviness of the moment may sometimes keep you from feeling assurance and comfort. He is still with you. Even when you feel empty inside. He is with you. Though you walk through the valley...

My flesh and my heart fail; But God is the strength of my heart and my portion forever. Psalm 73:26

Fear not for I am with you; be not dismayed, for I am your God; I will strengthen you, Yes, I will help you, I will uphold you with my righteous right hand. Isaiah 41:10

God's Holy Spirit has you in power, grace, and love. Your loved ones are in His presence now. They are safe in peace. They are free now, from all the tribulation of this world.

In my Father's house are many mansions; if it were not so, I would have told you. I go to prepare a place for you. And if I go and prepare a place for you, I will come again and receive you to Myself; that where I am, there you may be also. John 14:2-3

This mortal life is but a moment (within the scope of eternity).

In a moment, in the twinkling of an eye, at the last trumpet. For the trumpet will sound, and the dead will be raised incorruptible, and we shall be changed. For this corruptible must put on incorruption, and this mortal must put on immortality. So, when this corruptible has put on incorruption, and this mortal has put on immortality, then shall be brought to pass the saying that is written: "Death is swallowed up in victory." 1 Corinthians 15:52-54

Right now, life hurts more than anyone can ever know. You will get through this tragedy. Agony has swallowed your soul in an endless pit of emptiness. Your heart is broken. It may feel like razor-sharp swords stabbing you in the chest every morning; it may be paralyzing, pushing you down, and keeping you from getting up.

When you get up, your soul cries during the day. You are living with excruciating pain, seemingly unbearable.

Be easy on yourself. If you ever feel panic or anxious? Remember to take a moment to breathe. Take a deep breath, inhaling slowly. Exhaling slowly. Be conscious of your breathing. Breathe in peace. Breathe out anxiety. Breathe in strength. Breathe out fear. Breathe in love. Breathe out uncertainty. Breathe in life. Breathe out the emptiness. Breathe in love... Continue breathing. Inhaling slowly and exhaling slowly, until you feel calm.

In the midst of chaos, find moments to yourself to relax your mind and body. A relaxed mind is able to think more clearly. Take calm moments to yourself. It's important to get away from the "noise" of worldly concerns, and center yourself in peace. Especially if you are experiencing many intense emotions. Some of which might be anger, exhaustion, feeling overwhelmed, feeling inconsolable or feeling alone? I lift you up in peace. These are challenging times. You can have peace and make it through.

Reading something positive and uplifting may help ease the tension.

Even if you may not feel like reading anything at the moment? Reading scriptures will lift you up. Even just a few scriptures a day, to start, will bring life and refresh your soul.

At this moment, you may not know how you are going to go on living without your loved one's physical presence. Breathe peace with every breath you take. Your life matters, even though you may feel uncertain about facing the future? You can face anything. You can.

One breath at a time. One minute, one hour, one day at a time. You can live. You can live well.

Be easy on yourself. During initial stages of severe grief, sometimes, just being able to wash your face, is an accomplishment. Recognize your accomplishments. Be proud of the things you are able to do each day.

Making it through the tears of another lonely night, says you are victorious. Another day is before you, in this season of grief. This painful time will not last forever. This time will change, as the weather in seasons do. You will change. Growing into a season of healing, and better seasons ahead.

Chapter 1

To everything there is a season,
A time for every purpose under heaven

A time to be born, And a time to die; A time to plant, And a time to pluck what is planted; A time to kill, And a time to heal; A time to break down And a time to build up. A time to weep, And a time to laugh; A time to mourn, And a time to dance; A time to cast away stones, And a time to gather stones; A time to embrace, And a time to refrain from embracing; A time to gain, And a time to lose; A time to keep, And a time to throw away, A time to tear, And a time to sew; A time to keep silence, And a time to speak; A time to love, And a time to hate; A time of war, And a time of peace. Ecclesiastes 3:1-8

Strengthening Scriptures

When you pass through the waters, I will be with you; and through the rivers, they shall not overflow you. When you walk through fire, you shall not be burned, Nor shall the flame scorch you. Isaiah 43:2

Now may the God of hope fill you with all joy and peace in believing, that you may abound in hope by the power of the Holy Spirit. Romans 15:13

These things I have spoken to you, that in Me you may have peace. In the world you will have tribulation; but be of good cheer, I have overcome the world. John 16:33

Gratitude Stays Fresh with Every Season

During this grieving season and every season of your life, remember to be good to yourself and take care of your body. Giving your body what it needs to function well. Like drinking plenty of clean water, and other hydrating fluids.

At first, you may not feel like eating. When you feel like eating again. Eating foods high in nutritional value will help give you an extra boost. Resting when you can; living in gratitude one day at a time will help maintain stability and balance.

I can do all things through Christ who strengthens me. Philippians 4:13

And the Lord, He is the One who goes before you. He will be with you. He will not leave you nor forsake you; do not fear nor be dismayed. Deuteronomy 31:8

Likewise, the Spirit also helps in our weaknesses. For we do not know what we should pray for as we ought, but the Spirit Himself makes intercession for us with groanings which cannot be uttered. Now He who searches the hearts knows what the mind of the Spirit is, because He makes intercession for the saints according to the will of God. And we know that all things work together for good to those who love God, to those who are called according to His purpose. Romans 8:26-28

Just as when your loved ones were physically alive, they wanted what was best for you. Your loved ones still want what is best for you. Your peace and well-being in the days ahead are important to them. They want you to know they are in peace. They want to free your soul of worry. Put your burdens before The Lord. Feel free. Feel peace.

Cast your burden on the Lord, And He shall sustain you; He shall never permit the righteous to be moved. Psalm 55:22

Gift yourself with relaxing moments when you can smile at the good times you shared with your loved ones. Remembering your seasons together will keep their love for you front and center. Their everlasting love for you more pertinent than grief.

The memories and/or feelings of life's growing moments, learned during seasons with your loved ones, are yours. The memories and/or feelings of giving to each other your most precious gifts – yourselves, are yours. Nothing can ever take that away from you. Physical death did not take that away from you. Your love is still alive. Your love is everlasting.

And if your memory takes you back far enough, to a memory before mortality, you may remember your life is everlasting.

The reminder of everlasting life, and salvation in Jesus Christ, came clear to me during a season of unexpected tragedy. In this season, knowledge already in my soul, was confirmed in an experience I will always acknowledge. A reminder that everlasting life is real.

Chapter 2

The Christmas Season of 2003

The Christmas season of 2003 was the season that would precede the most unexpected seasons of our lives. In the middle of winter, I was gazing out a large window of our home, wondering if only icy frost could freeze frame a life. In the fullness of life, as we were. In the quiet of this moment, gratefulness filled my soul as I sat appreciating the view outside my window.

The view of snow-covered trees. One laced with Christmas lights in our front yard. A snowman with a carrot nose and raisins for his eyes and mouth, stood smiling. A little tunnel leading to an igloo the children excitedly built. I sat, simply gazing at this creation, and the mounds of snow several feet high, forming a barrier around our yard. The barrier – a result of commercial graders clearing neighborhood streets for traffic.

Mother Nature would continue to snow, making a fortress around our home, throughout long winter months ahead. A peaceful fortress. A quiet safe haven, away from the hustle and bustle of the world.

After coming in from playing outside in the snow, we shared the warmth from a stone fireplace, the warmth of loving hearts, and the warmth of drinking hot chocolate.

Hugs and laughter in this simple two-story home, gave us a feeling of living in grandness.

Big and grand, like nice, spectacular castles. The good ones in wonderful fairy tales. This feeling of a magnificent life came from the caring ways of how my husband treated me like a queen. His sons, each like a young prince and his daughter a princess. We meant the world to him, and he to us. Family, friends, and even strangers who became friends would share in the grandness of this unconditional love. As seasons came and went, like in other households, there were daily routines. The daily routines of work for mom and dad; school for children.

Summer months brought the daylight and midnight sun, shining almost 24 hours a day. There were neighborhood barbeques, and children passing through, stopping to play in the yard. Summer brought Anchorage alive. The sun kept people outdoors doing what they enjoyed doing. Things like hiking, biking, camping, gardening, sporting events, and many get togethers. As a family, we enjoyed these things as well.

Beautiful summers were some of the nice aspects of living in Alaska. For us, the little everyday things we shared was what made life Heaven on earth.

Moments, like sitting at the dinner table together. Eating, talking, laughing, and sharing our day.

With the change of seasons, came a change of sports – little league baseball and football. Though the names of teammates changed with each new season, good vibes remained the same. Cheering on the sidelines and taking turns at the snack shack. A close-knit community enjoying summer days.

Before we knew it, colors of the leaves were changing on the trees. Beautiful shades of purple, red, yellow, orange, and brown gave Anchorage a picturesque view. The leaves would fall from trees in time to fill large, orange Halloween bags for decorating the yard. We enjoyed Thanksgiving gatherings. We appreciated kind, cheerful neighbors spreading Christmas cheer by bringing over tasty, home baked fudge and cookies. December was our time for decorating the Christmas tree; hanging stockings, and trinkets by the fireplace. We loved living in our home. A home anyone could come to for support, peace and comfort in their time of need. Our home, a piece of Heaven on Earth. Such was life for us in the Last Frontier.

The Christmas of 2003 was different.

With gratitude, I was filling out Christmas cards, marveling at life's awesome moments when the phone rang.

A male voice on the phone introduced himself as Dr. Kelly. Dr. Kelly was calling from Alabaster Hospital in Alabama. He said my dad was in critical care and explained what needed to be done. I was shocked by the call because my dad hadn't told anyone he had cancer. Dad didn't want to worry anyone. He maintained a sunny disposition, and mostly gave words of encouragement, making everyone feel that everything was fine. I understood Dad's reasoning for not revealing what he was going through. He knew, had he told me, my siblings and I would drop whatever we were doing to be there for him. He wanted us to focus on living good lives; raising our families. I respected his reasoning, but still wish he had told me. He predicted my reaction correctly. In no time at all, my sisters and I left the states in which each of us resided and was in the hospital by his side.

In the critical care unit, in a barely lit room, dad opened his eyes in amazement that we were there. He smiled at the speed in which we arrived; happy to see us, comforted by our presence. We stayed, helping with whatever was needed. He was able to leave the hospital in time to spend Christmas day at home. We were blessed to share this valuable time together. After New Year's Day, my siblings and I went back to the states in which we lived.

The Start of a New Year

New Year's celebrations of 2004 and three months had gone by. Dad had planted tomatoes in his garden, similar to the garden he and mom planted together, when they lived in Alaska. They grew the most ripe, red, juicy, organic tomatoes I'd ever eaten. Moose roaming the neighborhoods stopped to feast on green vegetables from their lush garden. The moose enjoyed eating some of the plants grown with the love in which mom and dad put into their garden. Dad would be tending his garden in Alabama more this year, if his health allowed.

Spring was upon us in Anchorage, as well. The occasional smell of mildew from last year's dead grass uncovered by melting snow was being replaced by fresh scents of newly budding trees. Rolling streams of water sparkled in the sun, glistening down the edges of sidewalks. A mother moose whose two calves were newly born in our backyard a few years prior, came back.

Her babies were bigger now. They kept coming back every spring and summer, feasting on greenery, and resting under our deck.

Sometimes, the moose would look into the windows at us inside our home. We often smiled and waved at them, while respecting their peace and place in our back yard.

Important Note: Moose are gentle creatures, but they are also wild animals with natural instincts. Please do not ever approach a moose or any wild animal. You must stay a safe distance from wild animals at all times.

The School Year was Almost Over

The school year went great for each of our children. They enjoyed attending their schools – Susitna Elementary School and Wendler Middle School. Our 12-year-old son was present for each day of school throughout the entire year. He made a goal to be present for each day of classes and do his best in his studies. He accomplished his goal. There was also a nationwide incentive for children to have excellent attendance that year. Students who didn't miss 1 day of school, would receive a recognition certificate and be afforded an opportunity to go to Washington D.C. for a leadership conference and ceremony. My son wasn't as excited about the recognition or trip, as he was about self-realization in accomplishing a job well done. Our 8-year-old son enjoyed going to school as well. He especially enjoyed the activities and playing with his friends on the playground. Our 14-year-old daughter enjoyed middle school. She was excited to be going into her freshman year of high-school.

They were just as excited as many other children for upcoming summer fun; looking forward to a new school year ahead. My husband, Richard, was getting ready to pull his new motorcycle out of the garage. We were glad summer was here, so he could ride last year's birthday gift – his long- awaited motorcycle. He was so busy spending his hard-earned money taking care of me and the children, he waited to ride. A gift I wish he had long before.

With summer around the corner, it was time for him to ride…

Chapter 3

A Race with Time

During the past four months, Richard and I were figuring out how we could spend more time with dad while maintaining our jobs and life in Alaska.

Perhaps, we'd spend seasons in Alabama with him. We shared more phone conversations with dad.

We weren't ready for the phone call from Dr. Kelly. I could hear the compassion in his voice as he gently explained about the results of medical tests that showed dad had only two weeks left to live. The purpose of his call was to give us time to prepare. As I hung up the phone, I didn't know what to think. How does a person prepare for death, when you want so much for the ones you love to live? There was no time for death. Especially in the newness of life, of spring. Flowers were blooming. Baseball season was around the corner. A person just can't die before baseball season!

Dad wanted to watch his grandchildren play ball.

An hour glass, with sand pouring through its small middle opening was just one of many thoughts crowding my mind. At this point, time was not my friend. I knew I couldn't win a race with time. I wanted to try anyway. I wanted life to go on.

When Richard came home from work. I told him what Doctor Kelly told me. I would be getting permission from the children's school to take them out days before the school year's end. I wanted them to spend time with their grandfather. All their school work had been completed, which made me feel more confident about this necessary decision.

Everything was happening so quickly. My husband felt uncomfortable with his entire family leaving so suddenly. We have always been together.

"I just don't want you to go," he said.

He continued to comfort me by saying he understood we must go because my dad would be happy to see us and feel comforted by our presence. Our children would be spending precious time with their grandfather. He said he'd stay in Alaska to work; if we needed him to come, he would put in a request for leave from work, to join us.

The look on Richard's face seemed anxious, concerned, as though he was missing us already. I tried to relieve his concerns, and cheer him up.

I reminded him of how much time and energy he devoted to us daily. He freely gave of himself, his love.

He could look at this short time apart as a mini-vacation. He'd be free to relax, and enjoy doing anything and everything he ever wanted to do, without the responsibility of a family there. I tried to convince him of how much fun he could have with his free time. The concerned look on his face didn't change. He didn't even smile. He told me he wanted to spend his free time with us. Although, he understood that it was good to be with my dad during what may be his final days. He maintained his position that he didn't feel right about our family being apart at this time. He wanted us to come home as soon as we could. Knowing we'd miss him, I agreed. We'd return home as soon as we could.

Soon enough, my children and I, my sisters and their children, and my brother were all in Alabama. We were thankful to be able to be there.

Especially thankful that my youngest sister who was serving in the United States Army could be there. Servicemembers in her chain of command did what was needed to allow my youngest sister to be with her dad.

Her unit was about to be deployed for their second deployment to Iraq.

They were able to change her orders at the last minute, to a duty station in Alabama. We appreciated this very much. Dad, who was a retired, decorated, U.S. Army veteran, appreciated the staff at the Department of the Army who made this reunion possible. Possible to see his daughter one last time.

So much was happening. Each of us did all we could to make dad feel comfortable and loved more than ever before. I wanted to grant his desire to watch his grandchildren play baseball, and tried looking for a league starting the season early, with no avail. Settling with dad watching his grandchildren toss the baseball in the yard.

We bought the largest swimming pool we could construct and assembled it in the yard. One day the children were splashing around, laughing and playing in the pool. I thought the noise might be too much for dad.

When I asked my dad, he said he preferred hearing his grandchildren's laughter rather than silence. He really liked hearing his grandchildren's voices. It made him feel lively. It made him feel good.

Appreciating Life More Fully

Never before had I seriously considered genuine, spontaneous laughter as a sign of being truly alive. With Dad facing probable death, signs of life became more magnificent to me, regardless of how insignificant they seemed on a daily basis.

I noticed and appreciated more fully the signs of life.

Like birds chirping every morning. Their songs sounded clearer.

Crickets sounding off in the evenings, sounded more like nature's symphony to me.

One day, I noticed a peculiar, stray, gray cat that wondered into dad's yard. He seemed to just come, sit, and look up at me as I walked by him. He looked as if he was waiting for someone to feed him. I purchased cat food, and put the cat food on dad's porch so the cat could feed himself.

Then came a stray, black, puppy with curly locks. This puppy sat on dad's porch in a spot that made it obvious to notice him as I exited the front door. He looked like he needed some attention. I bought puppy chow from the store. Came back to dad's home and fed the dog. I washed the dog clean, and cared for him daily. Every day the dog would wag his tail, barking with joy, as he would come to greet me. As soon as things settled down, I planned to take him to a veterinarian for a checkup and do whatever was needed to bring him back to Alaska.

From the sounds of children laughing, to the sounds of nature; and the sights of little animals just showing up on dad's porch, signs of life seemed to be all around me.

Have you ever thought about the wonderous sights and sounds of life?

I wanted life to continue for my dad. I kept thinking positive thoughts, and prayed for Dad to be healed. I wanted my dad to become physically stronger again.

I conducted myself as though we would come back in future seasons to visit him. I purchased a nice used car to keep at dad's house for each time we'd come to visit in the future. I obtained a membership at a nearby gym. My sisters, brother and I each took care of everything dad needed or wanted. Dad didn't want much of anything. He just relaxed and enjoyed his time. I wanted positive thinking and positive actions to change the prognosis.

My sisters, brother and I were all researching cancer cures, natural remedies, medical procedures, or anything that could cure my dad.

We all wish we had known earlier, and wished we could have done more to help.

Dad's body was still in pain. He tried to hide the pain, steadily enduring medical procedures with confidence. Being with him during his appointments confirmed enormous strength he's shown all of his life. He stayed calm, composed and confident. I couldn't help but think of other times in his life when his bravery brought him through a battle. I remembered a conversation we had many years earlier.

Personal Battles and Actual Battles

Out of eagerness to learn and sincere curiosity, I would sometimes ask my dad about his experiences during the war in Vietnam. Many soldiers, many people on both sides of the war lost their lives. Dad rarely talked about what he experienced in Vietnam. One day I was wondering how a soldier could get any sleep at all while fighting on the front lines of battle.

I asked my dad how he could sleep.

He recalled an experience to me that explosions were going off everywhere. Artillery fire had hit soldiers, and their body parts were being torn apart in the heat of this battle. He was on the front lines. He told me they had to stay low in their foxholes that day. He tried to save a soldier's life next to him. The soldier did not survive his wounds.

Dad's somber answer to me, as to how a soldier could sleep on the front lines of battle was, "With dead soldiers beside us. It was hard. Especially, when we knew them. Especially, after doing all we could to keep them alive."

Then he became very quiet and appeared as though he did not want to talk about the war anymore. I respected he didn't want to talk about war, and appreciated his trust in me to share this part of his life on occasion. At least 23 times my dad was on the front lines. I couldn't begin to imagine the fearlessness and strength a war commanded from soldiers of his era.

Battles in People's Lives

The word battles came to mind. Various types of personal battles that we all face. The ones of a material, physical, emotional, or spiritual nature. I pondered the many ways each person has his or her own "cross to bear."

I pondered how some people who experience cancer may consider their experience with cancer as a battle, and if this experience was a battle for my dad?

Looking into my dad's eyes, I saw a man of complete confidence, assuring me "he's walked through fire" or fought "many battles" in his time, emerging victorious. Then, what occurred to me was perhaps his experience with cancer wasn't a battle for him after all. There was a special peace about him. He appeared certain and peaceful about everything.

Precious Moments

The two-week time frame projected by medical test results had passed. Many weeks later, time was gracious, allowing friends, relatives, and the pastor to come over for short visits. One of my dad's brothers, Uncle Joe, and his family flew in from Detroit. Dad was so happy to see them. They really enjoyed visiting with each other. Dad was in good spirits, making us laugh at times.

When he was able, he'd visit one of his favorite cousins – Louise – who lived down the street. She was 90 years old, intelligent and very wise. I enjoyed visiting with her too. Beautiful draperies, embroidered quilts, and precious pottery added a touch of elegance to priceless antique furniture in her home. Cousin Louise sewed, quilted, and made the pottery years earlier. I could feel the love, and genuine warmth of this space while we sat and talked for hours. Louise sat in her favorite chair sharing her life stories, our family history, and the history of what happened many years ago in Alabama.

One afternoon, while sitting with Cousin Louise, she told me dad talked with her about a vision he had of his mother.

"Your dad said he was out watering his tomato plants when he saw his mother standing in the yard. She was saying something to him." Louise paused for a few seconds. "Sometimes, when people are close to death; they see loved ones who have already passed on, calling them home."

In her 90 years, others who were nearing their time of death told her what they have seen or heard from loved ones who have passed on. Hearing dad's vision made her very sad because he was her favorite cousin.

"I don't want him to go..." she said, holding back her tears. "I'm gonna miss him... I'm praying the Lord will heal him..."

Hospice Help

Hospice representatives came to the house in the middle of May to deliver oxygen in case it was needed. Nurses brought medication and morphine, giving me instructions of how and when to administer it. Cancer, metastasized in final stages, can inflict severe pain on the human body.

Dad didn't want to take morphine. He remained calm in a peaceful state of mind. His strength was again, amazing to me.

Chapter 4

June 2004

Late in May and into June 2004, Dad was only drinking water and could barely keep it down. My sisters, brother and I stayed close, tending to whatever he needed during the days. I wanted to render help, if needed in the middle of the night, as well.

I grabbed a sleeping bag and slept half-awake on the floor in a corner of dad's room. Late one night as both of us were trying to sleep, he looked across the dimly lit room at me and quietly said, "Thank you, Brenda."

My mind filled with memories of many kind, caring, generous things he and my mother did for me, my sisters, and brother. I should be the one thanking him, I thought. I remembered in the 1970s at the age of 7 and 9, he brought orange slices to our room when my older sister and I had the chicken pox.

We didn't feel like making our way to the kitchen. So, we ate oranges on our brand-new canopy beds, with yellow and white matching blankets and laced pillows. Mom and dad probably spent more money than they would have liked on the canopy bedroom set, just because we really wanted it. Canopies were a popular item for little girls in the 1970s. Thoughts of how my parents patiently, lovingly, raised us over the years with such tremendous generosity. Their hard work and sacrifices for us to live a safe, secure, abundant life.

"Thank You, Dad," I replied. There was so much more I wanted to thank him for.

On June 2, 2004, late in the afternoon, my 2 sons and I were with my dad. Dad was lying in bed. His breathing different than previous days. Earlier in the week he insisted we only give him oxygen when he asked. He didn't want it forced on him. I just wanted to be absolutely sure he realized what he was requesting, knowing deep inside he wanted to be free to breathe his final breaths. I still gently eased the oxygen toward his face. He shook his head, no; mustering strength from his hand in a motion toward pushing the oxygen away. I looked into his eyes and understood completely. He wanted to freely breathe his final breaths in peace until his spirit left his body.

My two young sons and I were by his bedside.

I thanked my dad again, telling him we'd love him forever, assuring him we'd take good care of ourselves. One of my sons was holding his grandpa's hand. Grandpa looked at him…

"I am gonna be a great kid, Grandpa," my son said.

Grandpa smiled at him. Then peacefully, slowly looking toward the ceiling as if peering through to the heavens, he breathed his final breath.

We sat quietly with him… An unexplainable peace filled the room.

How did the seasons of our lives pass so quickly?

Not so long ago, I was only 3-years-old, going to my grandmother's funeral. I was walking with a procession of people down a dusty road toward our family cemetery, a historic cemetery in which our great, great relatives are buried. Great-grandparents, great-aunts, uncles, cousins, and now my dad would be buried there. Dad had been meticulously tending upkeep of our family cemetery for years.

In a few days, an honor guard from the military base would be here giving ceremonial respects to a distinguished U.S. Veteran, my dad. People from our community, friends and relatives would soon gather there. Overgrown branches of large, old trees surrounding the cemetery hung down and needed to be cut.

One hot summer day, my sister and I with a few landscapers were clearing away excess branches and shrubs on the outskirts of the cemetery. I was handing out water bottles, when panic came over me. An extremely uneasy feeling telling me it was urgent to return to Alaska. Was the heat getting to me? Was it a stress reaction from dad's passing? I wanted to act on this warning. For all logical purposes, everything was fine in Alaska.

One of my sisters, her son, my daughter, and my 12-year-old son had already returned home to Anchorage. We all missed my husband very much. My 12-year-old especially missed his dad. He was extremely eager to get home to be with his dad again. His little brother, missed his dad too.

I debated in my mind to send my 8-year-old back on the plane with his older brother. My 12-year-old was responsible and could have taken care of his little brother on their trip home. Had I known what would happen in the future, I would have sent him back to Anchorage on the plane with his brother so they could both be with their dad.

I was being cautious. Even though the airlines have representatives to accompany minors while changing planes, I did not want to take any chances. Just in case there was any slight probability of the boys being accidentally separated during the long trip. For safety reasons, I kept my 8-year-old in Alabama with me. If I could go back in time to make that decision again. I would have sent both our boys back to Anchorage together to be with their dad. I thought my 8-year-old and I could stay in Alabama to quickly finish what we needed to do there. We would immediately return to Alaska the very next day after my Dad's funeral.

Besides, the phone calls we were receiving from my husband were reassuring all was well at home. He told us about their activities, enjoying the warm Alaskan summer. Richard and our 12-year-old had fun at the movies. He loved and missed us, and couldn't wait until we were all together again. He asked if I needed him to fly to Alabama to help, and we could fly back together. Everything seemed happy back home.

Unexplained Feelings of Deep Sadness

Which is why I didn't understand this persistent, dreadful feeling in my soul. There was no apparent reason to feel such sadness and I didn't know where the feeling was coming from. I tried to ignore the sadness, and continued with final funeral and celebration of life preparations for my dad. My sister and I were at a local restaurant ordering food catering for guest. The final touches were almost complete.

The Curly-Haired Puppy

Another busy day almost over. My sister and I were driving back toward dad's house. As we were pulling into the long drive way, a neighbor lady who lived further up on dad's land was frantic, running toward our car.

"I'm sorry about the puppy," she said. "He just came running out... I'm so sorry. I'm so sorry."

She went on to explain, her daughter was driving around the corner. The puppy came running out. It was an accident.

There wasn't anything anyone could do for my little, black, curly-haired puppy. They buried him in the forest near our family cemetery.

Days earlier I was talking to my husband about bringing my new found puppy back to Alaska. My sister and I drove straight to the forest. As I sat down, weeping over the puppy, that dreadful, painful feeling in my heart and soul became stronger: I have to get out of here! I have to go home!

My head started hurting, every nerve in my body was shaken. Unexplainable sadness consumed me. Something felt very wrong.

I called home to check if everything was all right. I talked with my husband on the phone. He assured me everything was fine. Soon enough we'd be back together. Like always, his awesome sense of humor, understanding, and comforting words cheered me up. I couldn't wait to be back in his arms again.

Staying with Cousin Sabrina

We no longer needed to stay on dad's property. My 8-year-old and I wanted to visit with our cousin Sabrina, so we went to stay with her and her family. She, her husband, and children lived in a large, elegant, beautiful home in the country. Their children enjoyed playing with my son. They were kind, compassionate and fun-loving people. The atmosphere of their home felt safe, secure and happy. Still, overwhelming grief within me persisted, interrupting the few minutes of happiness I felt from being with such a wonderful family. This dreadful feeling grew stronger by the hour.

Sabrina noticed my nerves were visibly shaken.

Job in the Bible

The story of Job in the Holy Bible came to mind. Job was a faithful, righteous man living a life of abundance with his family and everything he could ever want.

Job loved God. Satan told God the only reason Job believed in him is because he has everything he has ever wanted. If everything Job cherished were to be taken from him, he would no longer honor God.

God knew Job would continue to honor him. Job faced one tragedy after another. Job endured physical, mental, and spiritual anguish. Through all of Job's severe pain and suffering, he remained steadfast in his faith. God blessed Job abundantly.

Although I didn't fully understand the story of Job. Recent events in my life were starting to feel like a Job story was starting to happen.

A day before my dad's scheduled funeral, my son and I, were in Sabrina's guest bed room. The room was beautiful. We sat on a king-size bed that had soft, plush comforters, and comfortable pillows.

The day prior, I enjoyed a phone conversation with my husband. He told me that he and everyone was doing fine in Alaska; he was excited that my son and I would be returning home soon. He reminded me to drink plenty of water and to please get some rest. I assured him I would rest.

The evening was getting closer to the time in which we were all going to sleep. Sabrina came into the guest-bed room just to say good-night. She stayed in the room and we talked for a little while. Our conversation was ending, and she was about to leave the room. As she started to leave the room. I sadly said:

"Sabrina. This is looking like a Job story to me."

"I certainly hope it isn't," she replied.

Then she walked slowly out of the room.

I was snuggled under the soft comforter trying to rest and perhaps get some sleep, when I heard the home phone ringing in another room. I thought Sabrina, her husband, and/or children were somewhere in the house, and would answer the phone, so I didn't get up to answer it.

I kept trying to keep my eyes closed. The telephone would stop ringing, then start ringing again. Their house was large. Maybe, they didn't hear the phone ringing, I thought. Could they all be outside? I felt a pressing need to answer the phone. If they didn't answer soon, I would get up to answer it. The phone just kept ringing.

Suddenly, Sabrina came rushing into the room, with the phone in her hand. "Brenda, it's a nurse from Providence Hospital in Alaska."

Sabrina handed the phone to me.

"Hello," I answered.

"Is this Mrs. Genaro?" asked a lady's voice on the phone.

"Yes, it is."

She said she was a nurse calling from providence hospital. "It's about your husband."

"Let me speak to my husband right now," I insisted.

"I'm sorry. He's passed."

"No."

I yelled in agony. I frantically ran out of the room, down the hall, and back again. My mind and body were in shock. There wasn't anywhere I could run or hide from the pain.

The nurse was still on the phone. I was trying to catch my breath and compose myself enough to at least continue the phone conversation.

Then I must have handed the phone back to Sabrina.

My son was alarmed at what was going on. He had been hearing the commotion, watching as tears flowed heavily down my face. He looked at me.

"Mommy. Is Daddy dead?" he asked, sadly, with a shocked, puzzled look on his face.

I didn't know what was happening. I just held him tightly in my arms.

We sat there in shock, quietly holding each other. We talked for a while.

Organizing thoughts in my head. As calm as I could, I said, "We have to get out of here. We need to find out what happened to dad."

I suggested he take a bath to get ready. We'd both get ready. I'd call for plane tickets.

"Well…" he replied, looking at his new suit on a chair. With his head bowed, walking slowly out of the room toward the bathroom, he added, "I guess, I'll wear the new clothes you bought me for grandpa's funeral to dad's funeral."

Chapter 5

Delayed in Alabama

The soonest available flight out of Alabama would not be leaving until 5:30 in the morning. We boarded Delta Airlines. As the plane was preparing for take-off, it was making strange noises. The pilot explained about experiencing technical difficulties. There was a problem with a computer chip, program, or something having to do with controlling the plane.

He said he was going to try a test run around the airport. If there weren't any more problems, we'd be able to make the hour and a half flight to Atlanta (our stop-over). During the plane's test run – circling the airport, the plane kept stalling, making sputtering noises. This was making me quite nervous.

I calmly raised my hand gesturing for the flight attendant to come my way. "Excuse me, ma'am. I'm not having a good week. My dad died. My dog died. A hospital nurse in Alaska called me last night, telling me my husband died suddenly. I have two young children in Alaska who don't know their father is dead yet, and I really have to get home to them. If this plane is not going to fly, please let me off," I requested with urgency.

"The safety of our passengers is of the pilot's utmost concern," she said unconvincingly.

As the plane kept sputtering. Other passengers looked concerned, as well. We were all relieved when the plane was again at a stand-still. The pilot said we were waiting for an expert or specialist to check out the problem. About an hour later, he advised passengers to de-board the plane. Passengers rushed off the plane like a stampede.

People were rushing everywhere, but their actions seemed to be happening in slow motion. Their voices seemed muffled and everything around me felt like a dream. All the passengers who deboarded were now looking for other departing flights. My son and I went from one airline to another trying to find available seats. A United Airlines ticketing agent must have noticed I was in distress. She listened intently to our desperate need to leave. She worked diligently, trying to make space available on any airlines. She kept trying. There just weren't any available seats. I must have fainted...

On the floor, I was looking up at my son holding my hand, and paramedics taking care of me. My son was talking to them. They were asking me questions. They wanted to take me to a hospital. They were trying to contact other family members. Everyone must have been attending my dad's funeral. If anyone had a cell phone, it would have been on silent or turned off. The "light-headedness" was going away, and I started breathing better.

After a while, the paramedics must have been convinced that hospitalization was no longer necessary. An airline employee called an airport shuttle for us. He rode with us to a nearby hotel, helped us check in, and walked us safely to our room. He was so kind, wanting to make sure we were all right. He offered his condolences, and left.

Later that evening, I called home to see how my other two children were doing. My 12-year-old said someone from the hospital called and was trying to get in touch with me. He told me his dad hadn't come home from the gym yet, and asked if I knew whether his dad was all right. I told him our flight was delayed and we'd be home soon.

Meantime, my son's friend called the hospital. A staff member accidentally revealed my husband had passed away.

A few minutes later my son called me back. "Mom. Someone from the hospital said dad is dead."

I didn't say anything. How could I? How could I tell him, his dad – his hero, his best friend in the whole world, was not coming home.

"Mom ?Mom?" he pleaded for answers.

"I'm coming home soon, son. Everything will be all right. I'll be there really soon."

I could hear the desperation in his voice. "Mom. Please. Just tell me." I kept reassuring him we'd be home soon.

"Is Dad dead? Please Mom. Just tell me."

My heart was breaking in a trillion pieces. A deep gut wrenching, aching sorrow sent a sick feeling up through my throat, mustering words in which I never thought I'd be telling a little boy. "Yes, son."

He let out an agonizing cry. The phone dropped. I heard what seemed as though he was hyperventilating.

I wanted to hold him and comfort him. I immediately called one of my best friends. Asking if she was able to rush over to our house. I called our next-door neighbor to rush to our house as well. They were shocked with the news. They had just seen my husband, riding his motorcycle the day before.

Early the next morning, I woke up in a fog. As though dreaming a very bad dream. The only person who was immediately real to me was my son. We went to the area where there was a continental breakfast. There were chairs and tables and people. We didn't feel like eating. My son was holding my hand, looking up at me every now and then, making sure I was all right. I was making sure he was all right, too. Being together was what mattered– that we were O.K., and getting on our flight for home. Home?

His dad wouldn't be picking us up at the airport.

Chapter 6

Arriving Home

I wanted to see my husband immediately upon arriving in Anchorage, but the medical examiner's office was closed for the weekend. My two children were waiting for us outside of our home when we arrived. I slowly walked through every room in our home. Everything was in its place. There was a large gold fish who grew so large, he now had a tank of his own, two large Oscars in an 80-gallon fresh water fish tank.

They had a routine, swimming to the edge of the tank at precisely the right time, waiting for Richard to feed them. A 60-gallon salt water metropolis was home to tangs, clownfish, and other sea friends swimming around a live coral reef.

Our furry little gerbils scurrying in their homes. Two cats relaxing on our living room floor.

The fish, the gerbils, the cats, our children, our friends, were where they were supposed to be. Except Richard. Where was Richard?

My friends were in our living room. Everyone seemed to have a stunned look about them. One of my best friends, Janet, and her daughter, Crystal, cooked delicious adobo and rice for us. There was an assortment of food nicely set on our dinner table. The table where Richard, me, and our children enjoyed talking and laughing almost everyday. Although, I knew Richard was gone, I still hoped to see him.

My friend, Cheryl spent many hours at our home. Sometimes, she'd just sit with me or hold my hand. Her compassionate, caring presence eased our grief. I felt better knowing she was there.

As the days went by, friends would come over just to say hello or see if we needed anything.

The children and I appreciated their outpouring of love and generosity. Gratefulness to them will be in my heart for the rest of my life.

O' Lord have mercy on me in my anguish. My eyes are red from weeping, my health is broken from sorrow. Psalms 31:9

One day, I went downstairs to our master bedroom to lie down, my heart and soul was mourning in agony. Heavy tears rolled down my face as I was crying out to my Lord and Savior.

"How could you!?" I asked. "I thought we were friends. Friends don't do things like that. Friends don't allow things like that to happen. Haven't we done everything you've asked? Richard was here for everyone. You didn't even give him a warning. Hurting me, I can understand. But, how could you hurt the children? Why?"

There was no holding back.

I had to tell God of my pain. On and on I cried. As I continued ranting and crying to God, a vision of The Virgin Mary entered my mind.

Yes. She suffered too. I somberly acknowledged in my mind the pain The Virgin Mary suffered at her son, Jesus's crucifixion and death for our sins.

The Gentle Reminder

My heart was broken and aching. My soul was crying. My eyes were crying. I lay there in mourning, crying, and missing my husband.

As I was crying, through my tears I saw a soft, bright, brilliant, illuminating, yellowish, whitish, goldish glow shaped like an oval almost as large as me. This brilliant glow was hovering on the ceiling, directly above me. Then, from somewhere, I clearly heard, "Have you forgotten?"

There was a pause.

"I am the resurrection and the life. Whoever believes in me shall not perish but have everlasting life. Your husband is not dead."

"Well, if he's not dead, take me to him," I demanded, pointing at the glow.

Oh wait, I thought. Not wanting to be struck dead to get there , I quickly clarified what I meant.

"I mean. Take me to him in Spirit. Where he is…So, I can talk to him, be with him," I politely asked.

"The time is not yet," this voice answered.

Suddenly, it dawned on me I was talking to this brilliant glow. Wait a minute. I thought. Why was there a glow up there anyway? Wiping my tears, I was staring intently at the glow trying to figure out where it was coming from. The sun wasn't shining, and the ceiling was white when I left for Alabama. Besides, this glow was moving.

With my children needing me to raise them, it was the wrong time to start seeing things. So, I got out of bed and checked our walls just in case it had been painted yellow somewhere, while I was gone, and the reflection was somehow making this glow. I had to find a logical answer to this brilliant glow.

Thoroughly, I inspected the walls and all of my surroundings. Everything was the same as before I had left for Alabama. So, I lay back down on my bed. The glow was still hovering on the ceiling. I tried to sleep. I would peep up at the ceiling every now and then just to see if the glow was still there. Several times, I saw the glow was still there, gently hovering, gently comforting me. The glow stayed with me all night. I fell asleep. When I woke up in the morning, the glow was gone. I felt an energy helping me get up out of the bed. This gentle energy helped me feed our fish in the fish tank.

In the days following, I shared my experience with people who were close to me. I wrote my experiences down on paper and composed a large portion of this book in 2004 and 2005.

Now, in 2021, looking back on that experience. I realize I could have probably continued communicating in that particular moment with "The Brilliant Glow," which caught me by surprise. Had my finite mind immediately comprehended and grasped the infinite reality of the communication. The sacred communion with The Holy Spirit, reminding me that everlasting life is real. I am confident, God, His Holy Spirit communicates with each of us in various ways. Ways that are unique and personal.

The Holy Spirit Scriptures

However, when He, the Spirit of truth, has come, He will guide you into all truth; for He will not speak on His own authority, but whatever He hears He will speak; and He will tell you things to come. He will glorify Me, for He will take of what is Mine and declare it to you. All things that the Father has are Mine. Therefore, I said that He will take of mine and declare it to you. John 16:13-15

But the Helper, the Holy Spirit, whom the Father will send in My name, He will teach you all things, and bring to your remembrance all things that I said to you. Peace I leave with you, My peace I give to you; not as the world gives do I give to you. Let not your heart be troubled, neither let it be afraid. You have heard Me say to you, 'I am going away and coming back to you.' If you loved Me, you would rejoice because I said, 'I am going to the Father; for My Father is greater than I. "And now I have told you before it comes, that when it does come to pass, you may believe. I will no longer talk much with you, for the ruler of this world is coming, and he has nothing in me.

But the world may know that I love the Father, and as the Father gave Me commandment, so I do. Arise, let us go from here.
John 14:26-31

And I will pray the Father, and He will give you another Helper, that He may abide with you forever – the Spirit of truth, whom the world cannot receive, because it neither sees Him nor knows Him; but you know Him, for He dwells with you and will be in you. I will not leave you orphans; I will come to you. John 14:16-18

But when the Helper comes, whom I shall send to you from the Father, the Spirit of truth who proceeds from the Father, He will testify of Me. John 15:26

And this is the promise that he has promised us – eternal life. 1 John 2:25

...that having been justified by His grace we should become heirs according to the hope of eternal life. Titus 3:7

God is Spirit, and those who worship Him must worship in spirit and truth. John 4:24

Jesus said to her, "I am the resurrection and the life. He who believes in Me, though he may die, he shall live. And whoever lives and believes in Me shall never die. Do you believe this?" John 11:25-26

And the Word became flesh and dwelt among us, and we beheld His glory, the glory as of the only begotten of the Father, full of grace and truth. John 1:14

Now on the first day of the week, very early in the morning, they, and certain other women with them, came to the tomb bringing the spices which they had prepared. But they found the stone rolled away from the tomb. Then they went in and did not find the body of the Lord Jesus. And it happened, as they were greatly perplexed about this, that behold, two men stood by them in shining garments. Then, as they were afraid and bowed their faces to the earth, they said to them, "Why do you seek the living among the dead? He is not here, but is risen! Remember how He spoke to you when He was still in Galilee, saying, 'The Son of Man must be delivered into the hands of sinful men, and be crucified, and the third day rise again.'"

They remembered His words. Then they returned from the tomb and told all these things to the eleven and to all the rest. Luke 24:1-9

Eternal Life Scriptures

...but has now been revealed by the appearing of our Savior Jesus Christ, who has abolished death and brought life and immortality through the gospel. 2 Timothy 1:10

...so that as sin reigned in death, even so grace might reign through righteousness to eternal life through Jesus Christ Our Lord. Romans 5:21

Jesus spoke these words, lifted up His eyes to heaven, and said: "Father, the hour has come. Glorify Your Son, that Your Son also may glorify You, as You have given Him authority over all flesh, that He should give eternal life to as many as You have given him. John 17:1-2

...in hope of eternal life which God, who cannot lie, promised before time began. Titus 1:2

For we know that if our earthly house this tent, is destroyed, we have a building from God, a house not made with hands, eternal in the heavens. For in this we groan, earnestly desiring to be clothed with our habitation which is from heaven. 2 Corinthians 5:1-2

Whereas you do not know what will happen tomorrow. For what is your life? It is even a vapor that appears for a little time and then vanishes away. James 4:14

The moments in which we live and breathe are all we have. The moments at hand, which we can choose to honor God, love ourselves, and love others. Not knowing what tomorrow holds.

Chapter 7

Sometimes Life Ends Abruptly

When my husband was in his early twenties, he was in college, taking an English class. One of the class assignments was a free-writing journal. I'm sharing a few pages from his journal...

Sure, is amazing how fast things really do happen. Wow it just seems like yesterday that I was still a child and living with my parents and going to school playing sports. Just being a kid. It just shows you how short one's life on this earth so I guess we should make the best of it.

My philosophy of life is somewhat simple. In my terms: Life is very short if you sit down and really think about it. Considering that geographers and geologist have estimated that earth is approximately 4.8 billion years old. When I took a class out at Elmendorf Geography and learned how long it takes for most acts of nature such as the making of mountains, lakes, oceans, forest and continents it sure made me feel that my eighty years or so of my life on this planet is like being a drop of water in an endless sea.

As I have gotten older and have been to different places and have experienced other cultures, I have realized that I am a very fortunate person to be an American Citizen with rights and unlimited opportunities. I count my blessings every day. We all should try to reach our goals that we have set and work hard to accomplish them.

And if you get knocked down, just get up and wipe yourself off, and try again. There will always be people out there with piss poor attitudes that like to tell you that you are not capable of reaching your goals. These are people that allowed others to mold their lives for them and not allow themselves to reach their dreams.

If you look at most successful people or read a book on someone's success story. They usually tell you about individuals who said they would never amount to anything. I use negative people to positively change me. It just makes me more intent on reaching my goals. In the world today you have to look out for yourself and go out and get what you want.

Because I personally don't want to be the one who is sittin in a rockin chair and saying I should have done this and I should have done that…. just do it. Winners never quit and quitters never win. (Richard Alan Genaro, Free Style Writing, Journal Entry # 14 English 111, University of Alaska Anchorage)

***

Why are fathers so proud of their new born babies?

Becoming a father is something very special to me.

It's such an amazing event to watch the process of my wife's pregnancy. Not only the physical aspects but the emotional changes as well, not so much the emotional ones. I have experienced some changes as well, not physical ones of course but emotional ones. At first when I found out my wife was pregnant; I will have to admit I had mixed emotions.

First, I was scared and then I was happy. These feelings kind of counteracted each other the whole nine months of her pregnancy. The scared feeling that I was experiencing came to an abrupt end when my wife gave birth to a 7 lb. 11oz. baby girl. It's kind of hard to explain your feelings when you have the opportunity to witness something as amazing and wonderful as birth.

This whole event was very stressful for both of us, and also very physically draining much more so for Brenda. This is something that I will remember for the rest of my life. It's all worth it when you see the baby and get to hold her for the first time. I will have to admit sometimes it's hard to always keep a positive attitude when our little bundle of joy decides that she would like to have her diaper changed and maybe have a little bit of warm milk. Sometimes she might decide that she feels like staying up for a few hours or so, this is not so bad if it is in the evening.

But sometimes she would like to do this at 2 a.m. in the morning. These are all just small obstacles that can be overcome with patience and some understanding. Babies are so innocent and pure and so very much dependent on their parents. It's hard to think that someday this tiny child will grow up and go to college, get married not necessarily in that order, and maybe have children of her own.

Sure, is amazing how fast things really do happen. Wow it just seems like yesterday that I was still just a child and living with my parents and going to school playing sports. Just being a kid. It just shows you how short one's life on this earth so I guess we should make the best of it. (Richard Alan Genaro, Free Style Writing, Journal Entry # 2, English 111, University of Alaska Anchorage)

The part in which Richard wrote about getting older, and someday sitting in a rocking chair, stood out to me. "The rocking chair" used as a symbol of a place for reflective thinking. Richard's journal entries show he had expected to live a long, happy, productive life. A life in which he thought we would have grown older and wiser together, and could someday reflect back on a life well built. He was shocked at the sudden timing of his physical death. We were all shocked. The medical examiner was shocked too.

She said, "When I first saw your husband at the hospital, my jaw just dropped. He looked like a perfect superman. I couldn't believe this person was dead. We ran extensive tests. All of his organs were perfect. Organs of an exceptionally healthy man. He had zero percent body fat. Well, not exactly zero percent. I mean, just the perfect amount of body fat to keep an exceptionally healthy person, healthy. We could tell he ate well and exercised. Even his heart was healthy, with the exception of the little bubble that burst, an aneurism. It was a coronary aneurism in which the exact cause is unknown. He was really, exceptionally healthy."

We continued to talk. She again told me how shocked she was at his death, and kept repeating how exceptionally healthy he was.

A couple of hours before Richard died, he was telling my daughter to have fun at a baseball game, and my son how he'd take him and his friend "go-carting" that weekend. He said he was going to the gym and would be back in a couple hours.

Most people do not know the "hour" in which life, as they know it, will end. The end of life is not what most people think about. For if they did, nothing would ever get done. Most people have plans, keep schedules, calendars, or something written or in their mind as to how they want their future to come about.

Sometimes or sadly, plans change. Physical death happens, sometimes when least expected, bringing trauma, tears and grieving. While grieving, the time we have to share with those who are still alive is still not guaranteed. Tomorrow is not promised to anyone. What matters is today. Each day you are alive matters. Every time you breathe matters. Breathe life. Speak life into your situation.

Please trust that your grief will end. Your circumstances will change for the better. Everything changes. The good seasons in our lives, that we wish could last forever, change. The tragic seasons in our lives, that we wish never happened, change. This you already know. You will grieve in your own way, in your own time.

Look at the birds of the air; they do not sow or reap or store away in barns, and yet your Heavenly Father feeds them. Are you not much more valuable than they? Matthew 6:26 NIV

Power and Faith Scriptures

The following scriptures have helped give me strength through tough times. I hope you find strength in them, and other scriptures in the Bible.

I can do all things through Christ who strengthens me. Philippians 4:13

The Lord is my strength and song, And He has become my salvation. Psalm 118:14

My soul melts from heaviness; Strengthen me according to your word. Psalm 119:28

My flesh and my heart fail; But God is the strength of my heart and my portion forever. Psalm 73:26

But You, O Lord, do not be far from Me; O My Strength, hasten to help Me! Psalm 22:19

He gives power to the weak, And those who have no might He increases strength. Even the youths shall faint and be weary, And the young men shall utterly fall, But those who wait on the Lord Shall renew their strength; They shall mount up with wings like eagles, They shall run and not be weary, They shall walk and not faint. Isaiah 40:29-31

The Lord will give strength to His people; The Lord will bless His people with peace. Psalm 29:11

The Lord is my strength; He will make my feet like deer's feet, And He will make me walk on my high hills. Habakkuk 3:19

Have I not commanded you? Be strong and of good courage; do not be afraid, nor be dismayed, for the Lord your God is with you wherever you go. Joshua 1:9

Fear not, for I am with you; Be not dismayed, for I am your God. I will strengthen you, Yes, I will help you, I will uphold you with My righteous right hand. Isaiah 41:10

Finally, my brethren, be strong in the Lord and the power of His might. Ephesians 6:10

Chapter 8

Sometimes, it seems like life presents one challenge after another. Even so, during times of grief. Under extreme stressful conditions, relying only on your own strength may become exhausting and overwhelming. Giving your load to God will help you. He will help you carry the "the cross" you are bearing. Lean on the Lord. Give your burdens to Him. How do we give our burdens to the Lord?

By accepting that you do not have all the answers. In certain situations, telling God that you do not know what to do. Surrendering your life to Him, and ask Him to lead you. Open your door – your heart, soul, mind, and spirit – to accept His guidance. Then, be still, if needed, to hear His voice. Read the Holy Scriptures. God speaks to each one of us in a way that is unique to each one's understanding. Many times, it is through the scriptures.

Trust in God

Our human nature tends to take the burdens back, when we feel Our Lord is not acting fast enough. We want to fix things. We don't want to be in pain, or those we love to be in pain. Keep trusting.

Trust in the Lord with all your heart, and lean not on your own understanding; In all your ways acknowledge Him, And He shall direct your paths. Proverbs 3:5-6

Now it happened, on a certain day, that He got into a boat with His disciples. And He said to them, "Let us cross over to the other side of the lake."

And they launched out. But as they sailed, He fell asleep. And a windstorm came down on the lake, and they were filling with water, and were in jeopardy. And they came to Him and awoke Him, saying, "Master, Master, we are perishing!"

Then He arose and rebuked the wind and the raging of the water. And they ceased, and there was calm. But He said to them, "Where is your faith?"

And they were afraid, and marveled, saying to one another, "Who can this be? For He commands even the winds and water, and they obey Him!" Luke 8:22-25 NKJV

Holy, Holy, Holy Lord, Prayer

Hear our cries. Forgive our sins. This pain seems too much to bear.
We come to you with heart and soul in hand.
Giving our lives to you, Lord.
Help us now Dear God.
Help us breathe again.
Breathe in Life, in the midst of darkness.
Help us see again. Clearly see our way.
Meet our needs every day,
and uphold us in your mighty way.
Grant us peace.
Thank you for the precious Blood of your Son,
Jesus Christ – our victory over dark forces.
In you we have victory over death.
In you we have victory in this life.
Thank you for the resurrection.
Thank you for salvation.
Thank you for everlasting life.
In Jesus Christ.
Amen

Chapter 9

Create a Space of Peace in Your Mind

One of the things I did was create a special space for meditation in my home. I decorated a small space – a space of tribute to my husband – just for me. In it, I placed a few of my husband's favorite things, and a few things that meant a lot to our family. This was my space of gratitude and relaxation. In this space, I would read scriptures, write in my journal, draw or paint pictures. I would listen to uplifting music. Sometimes I would cry in this space, too. Perhaps, you may want to create a space that is soothing, uplifting, and relaxing for you? A place that's enjoyable. A place that makes you smile. This space can be as big or small as you would like. If you do not have a house, an apartment, or roof over your head? You can create this space where ever you are. You can always create this space of peace in your mind. In fact, having peace in your mind is what counts.

Essential Oils

There are natural methods used to help lift your mood, or create a peaceful, relaxing atmosphere. Essential oils are helpful. Essential oils are natural oils typically obtained by distillation. Their characteristics come from the fragrance of the plants or other sources which they have been extracted. You can purchase essential oils in natural health food stores, some grocery stores, retail outlets, or online. Use only pure, organic, or therapeutic grade oils for best results. You can put the oil in a diffuser according to the directions. This will put the essence of the oil in the air and evoke feelings of wellness associated with particular oils.

Some people have found oils such as orange, lemon, or peppermint to be uplifting. Lavender, chamomile, frankincense, and rose can evoke feelings of relaxation. Essential oils can be used for many different purposes as well. Choose oils that agree with you, and make you feel good.

If you do not have an essential oil diffuser, you can put some oil on a piece of cloth to smell the scent. (Please do not apply any essential oil, by itself, directly on your skin or any part of your body. Please do not ingest essential oils.)

Essential oils must be combined with carrier oils to be safely applied to your skin, according to proper usage. Carrier oils are oils like coconut, almond, olive and jojoba. After mixing the essential oil of your choice to a carrier oil of your choice. You can apply it to your skin. This pampers your skin and may feel comforting, as you care for your body.

Bach Flower Essence

Another good remedy is Bach Flower Essence. Bach Flower Essence Remedies were developed in England in the 1930s by Dr. Edward Bach. Dr. Bach was widely recognized as an outstanding bacteriologist. He was a homeopathic doctor with many skills and talents. Although, he was trained in conventional medicine, he wanted to find the main causes of disease. He intuitively knew the physical symptoms he was treating in his patients were related to emotional and mental conditions. He understood the soul or spirit dimensions of healing. He wanted a natural, non-toxic way in treating the inner levels of the human experience. Dr. Bach's extensive research and dedicated work lead him to develop the Bach Flower Remedies. These remedies are now used all over the world.

The Bach Flower Essence called Rescue Remedy is used for times of shock, stress and/or trauma. The Bach Flower Essence called Star of Bethlehem is used for neutralizing grief, stress and trauma. These natural remedies are not an overnight fix. Rarely is there anything that has an instantaneous healing effect.

Many people who have used Bach Flower Remedies have said the remedies gently work on a deeper human level, helping with things like awareness, insight, and discovery of the human potential along their journey of grief. I have used both Rescue Remedy and Star of Bethlehem during certain seasons in my life with good results. This may be something you'd like to discover. You may want to educate yourself about these remedies to discover which ones may be helpful for you.

Eating Well

During initial stages of grieving, many people lose their appetite. Eating may not be appealing at a time of initial grief. Most people do not or can-not eat at first. I did not feel like eating at first. I could barely drink water and other juices. Staying hydrated is helpful. Drink plenty of clean water. Perhaps, when you are able to think of food you really enjoy eating, the thought may initiate your taste buds to want to eat again.

After gaining your appetite back. Eating foods with high nutritional value will help your body feel healthier.

Juicing Vegetables and Fruits

Eating more vegetables and fruits is a good way to put nutrition in your body. Years ago, I started juicing some of my fruits and vegetables. If you have not juiced fruits and vegetables before, I believe juicing is something you will really enjoy. You must have a juice extractor (juicer) to extract the juice from fruits and vegetables.

Basic juice extractors are sold at some retail stores, like Walmart, Fred Meyer, or Costco. Thrift stores sometimes sell barely, used juice extractors that still work well. You may want to educate yourself on the many different brands of extractors, to choose the one that is best for you. You can also order excellent quality juice extractors on line through the internet. Some excellent quality extractors cost more money. Purchase the juicer that suits your purposes. I use a Breville Juice Extractor that works well for me. There are other brands that work extremely well also.

Put your juicer on a countertop or clean, stable surface. Make sure the juicer is clean. Wash your vegetables and/or fruits. Chop the vegetables and/or fruit. According to the directions, turn on the juicer. Put the vegetables or fruit in the juicer. The juicer will extract the juice into the designated container, cup, or glass. Drink the delicious, nutritious juice. Drinking the juice immediately provides the best nutrients.

Would you like to learn more about adding vegetables to your eating choices, or eating plant-based foods?

If you are not already familiar with eating plant-based. There are excellent, knowledgeable doctors who teach on eating plant-based, and live what they teach. I am mentioning a few names of experts in this area of nutritious eating, to get you started:

• Dr. T. Colin Campbell Ph.D.
• Dr. John A. McDougall, M.D.
• Dr. Caldwell Blakeman Esselstyn Jr., M.D.

Many people have found eating more plant-based foods makes them healthier, stronger, and more energetic.

What do you allow in your life?

Are you selective of what you allow into your life?

If you would like to be grounded, and be in a more positive frame of mind – be selective at what you allow in your life. Even regarding what you see and hear. Listen to things that are uplifting for you. Uplifting music, movies, talks, speeches, or good sermons that are inspired by men or women of God who are led by the Holy Spirit.

In Anchorage, I enjoyed listening to the uplifting sermons of Pastor Ivery L. Henderson in his Anchorage, Alaska services. Pastor Henderson's sermons were being led by the Holy Spirit. Pastor Henderson spoke of the unconditional love of Jesus Christ, love for each other, faith, service to others, empowerment, gratitude and many more topics with a deeper and more profound meaning. He exemplifies what he preaches in his everyday life.

In your area, or on the internet, there may be sincere, inspirational people who you may want to listen to for positive encouragement along your journey in life.

Sometimes, I listen to sermons from pastors such as Pastor Cora Jakes Coleman, Pastor Sarah Jakes Roberts, and Pastor Ron Carpenter online. Their sermons have been a source of positive encouragement for me. Listen to the people and the sermons in which the Holy Spirit guides you, for particular messages at particular times in your life.

Health Check-Ups

Continue with routine health physicals, dental checkups, or eye-exams, if needed. Stress can affect our bodies in many ways. Getting a physical may bring awareness to a condition in which you may not be aware. Or give you peace of mind regarding any symptoms you may be experiencing. A physical may also be beneficial if you are starting a new exercise program.

Exercise

When you have the strength, and are able to exercise, do exercises you enjoy. Walking is a good, simple exercise. Walking helps keep the mind and body balanced.

More...

Engage in safe, positive activities that make you feel better. Uplifting activities like listening to good music, listening to enlightening sermons, or listening to the sounds of nature. You can watch funny movies to make you laugh. You can read books, or write your own book. You can create your own art. You can start a new hobby. Build model airplanes or cars. Work on vehicles. Repair or update old objects or furniture. Take pictures. Discover the photographer in you. Draw, paint, sculpt, sew, quilt. Discover the artist in you. Try cooking or baking a new recipe. Discover the chef in you. Create a new computer program. Discover the genius in you.

Browse hobby stores, thrift stores, or antique stores. Go to a museum. Take walks for exercise. There is more safety in numbers when walking through nature's wilderness, parks, or preserves.

You may be able to enjoy nature in your own yard or immediate surroundings. Plant a garden. Nurture an indoor plant. Organize your home. Learn a new exercise or dance. Write a letter to a family member or friend. Whether you send the letter or not. Write a letter to yourself. Start a new interesting project. Finish a project you always wanted to finish. The list can go on with the things you would like to do. Be kind to yourself and enjoy what you are doing.

There are other reasons for staying positively engaged in worthwhile activities. Yes, for relaxation and for fun. More importantly, being active helps in maintaining healthy balance in your life.

If you are not in a position to do any of those things for any reason, you can still maintain PEACE in your mind. Peace in your mind is what counts.

You can have peace by recalling or remembering positive, uplifting events in your life. Grasp the good feelings you felt during those times. Hold those wonderful thoughts, emotions, feelings, or accomplishments in your mind. Allow the good vibes to spread in your mind and all over your body. Think about inspiring words, songs, or sermons you have heard or read. Think about sincere, nice things someone has said to you or says to you.

Keep the goodness of wholesome, uplifting, things you have experienced or was said to you in the forefront of your mind. In your current circumstances, keep in mind, you are valuable and unique. You have much to give the world. Keep in mind, God's love for you.

Consciously block out negative things or comments. Don't let negatives enter your mind. If a negative enters, delete it right away and replace this space with positive thoughts. Get ahold of the Holy Scriptures, and read the Word of God. The Word of God will bring life to your soul and peace to your mind.

Stay focused on God, and on positive things. Keep yourself uplifted. Even while grieving, keep your mind in a good safe, space as much as you can. As natural, and human as it is to grieve; there is warning in grieving for long periods of time.

Scriptures for Maintaining Your Peace

Grieving that lasts for long periods of time will take its toll on your mental, physical, and spiritual health. When conditions of grieving, depression, discouragement, despondency, or hopelessness last for long periods of time; the enemy will take advantage of this human weakness.

Be vigilant. Periods of weakness are times when the enemy sneaks influence into a person's life, sometimes, without that person realizing it. The enemy's tactics are concealed and sneaky. The enemy has taken advantage of people from the beginning of time. At one point, the enemy – Satan– tried to take advantage of Jesus:

Then Jesus was led up by the Spirit into the wilderness to be tempted by the devil. And when He had fasted forty days and forty nights, afterward He was hungry. Now when the tempter came to Him, he said, "If you are the Son of God, command that these stones become bread."

But He answered and said, "It is written, 'Man shall not live by bread alone, but by every word that proceeds from the mouth of God.'" Then the devil took Him up into the holy city, set Him on the pinnacle of the temple, and said to Him, "If you are the Son of God, throw Yourself down. For it is written: 'He shall give His angels charge over you,' and 'In their hands they shall bear you up, Lest you dash your foot against a stone.'"

Jesus said to him, "It is written again, 'You shall not tempt the Lord your God.

Again, the devil took Him up on an exceedingly high mountain, and showed Him all the kingdoms of the world and their glory. And he said to Him,

"All these things I will give You if You will fall down and worship me."

Then Jesus said to him, "Away with you Satan! For it is written, You shall worship the Lord your God, and Him only you shall serve.'"

Then the devil left Him, and behold, angels came and ministered to Him. Mathew 4:1-11

Be sober, be vigilant; because your adversary the devil walks about like a roaring lion, seeking whom he may devour.1 Peter 5:8

Chapter 10

Take care of yourself, especially during stressful times. The pandemic that started in 2020 has affected people's lives all over the world. If you were already experiencing hardships, the pandemic added to these struggles. The death of a loved one, your loved one, during these tough times is devastating.

In their final hours, your loved one could feel your love, even though you were not physically by their side. They knew you wanted to be physically with them, and felt your comforting energy near them.

That's what love is. That's what love does. In our physical absence, love touches our loved ones, letting them know we are there for them.

Your loved ones are no longer suffering in their physical bodies. They are in the glory of God. They are free. They want you to be free, also. Free from worry, free from anxiety, free from pain. Close your eyes and feel free.

Feel love. Feel free. Take a deep breath in – breathing in freedom and love. Breathe out anxiety and pain. Take a deep breath in – breathing in freedom and love. Breathe out worry and pain. Continue taking slow deep breaths. Calming, soothing, freeing.

Close your eyes. See clear blue, wondrous skies. Imagine yourself floating like soft, white, fluffy clouds. See an eagle soaring high, high, high into the sky. You are that eagle soaring high. Soaring free. Your loved ones smile when you feel free. Smile, because someday you'll see them again.

We are living in challenging times. Sometimes we are just getting up from one hardship, just to be side swiped by another. It may sometimes feel as though we are continuing to pick ourselves up, over and over again.

There are times when people do all the natural things they can do, like, eating right, exercising, natural therapies, and even prayer. But still, due to overwhelming circumstances, or an imbalance in our mind or body, depression or anxiety takes its toll.

Is seeking professional help what you may need?

During overwhelming circumstances, it may be beneficial to see a good, intuitive doctor. A knowledgeable doctor who can diagnose whether the symptoms you are experiencing are because you are naturally grieving. Or if you are experiencing anxiety, clinical depression or other mental or physical conditions.

Use Medication Responsibly when Needed

Keep in mind, grieving causes symptoms you may not have experienced prior to the physical death of your loved one. Some or all of these symptoms may be temporary due to grief, and may subside as time passes.

A good, knowledgeable doctor can prescribe medication if your current condition requires the help of medicine. This is a decision that must be done with careful consideration and good judgment. You must do what is best for you.

If you are prescribed medication for your condition? And you decide to take the prescribed medication? Educate yourself about your current condition. Familiarize yourself with the medication, uses, and probable side effects. Communicate the symptoms you are feeling with your doctor. If needed, continue with follow up appointments. Continue to take good care of yourself.

No matter the tragedy, or the sufferings you face, never abuse prescription drugs, street drugs, or alcohol. Abusing these substances will only make life worse. Even if it feels the effects are temporarily relieving your pain.

This temporary relief is only an illusion. Do not try to escape from pain by using drugs. This only causes more pain for you and everyone who loves you. While the drug or the effects of the drug is in control, you may end up doing something harmful. Something in the spur of the moment that will destroy your life or someone else's life forever. On drugs, or coming down off of drugs, you may end up doing something you will regret for the rest of your life. Something you would have never done, had you been sober. Be sober. Think clearly. Think well into your future.

Long term drug or alcohol abuse changes the chemistry, structures, and/or patterns of cells in your brain. Abuse effects other organs as well. Drug addiction is also an open access door for Satan to enter and cause destruction in your life.

Scriptures for Staying Vigilant

The thief does not come except to steal, and to kill, and to destroy. I have come that they may have life, and that they may have it more abundantly. John 10:10

Lest Satan should get an advantage of us: for we are not ignorant of his devices. 2 Corinthians 2:11

Healing from Addiction (Stay Free to Live Your Life)

If you do not want to be a slave, in bondage to Satan's every whim, you will completely avoid drugs! It is an open door to destruction.

Satan will use drugs to destroy you and everything and everyone that means anything to you. Stay away from drugs and stay free. Stay free in your mind and body. Stay free in your life.

Stay free to live your life – a great life.

If you are currently using drugs or alcohol, do whatever you need to do to stop using. Get out of it. Even if it's the most difficult thing you will do or have ever done. Stop using. Get help. You can do it. You can live clean and sober. There are caring people all over the world who are praying for you. We are praying for your sobriety. Praying for your freedom. You have the ability to free yourself. You have the ability to be free.

I know you are hurting, and seriously recognize the pain you are going through:

- The substance(s) you are using, or were using, caused altered changes in your brain and body that severely affected your thought patterns and/or functions in your body.
- The changes in your brain and body makes withdrawing from these substances extremely painful. Take care and use caution. Withdrawals sometimes cause agitation and cause undesirable thoughts and actions. Depending on the substance, withdrawals may sometimes be life threatening and require the help of a professional, medical detox facility.
- Please do what you can to educate yourself on the effects of these dangerous substances. If needed, please seek help and admit yourself to a good, professional, medical, detox facility or treatment center.
- If there are long waiting lists to be accepted to a good medical facility where you live, don't give up. Put your name on the list. Still, make it a goal to stop using.
- Tell a responsible person who you know and trust that you are trying to stop using. This is so that this responsible, caring person can be aware of your situation and help you, keep an eye on you, or check on you to assure your safety and well-being.
- If decreasing the amount of usage slowly, at first, is what it takes? Decrease the amount of usage, while seeking professional help. Try hard to stop. Replace negative thoughts in your brain, with positive, uplifting thoughts. It will take time to heal your brain. YOU CAN HEAL YOUR BRAIN. YOU CAN HEAL YOUR MIND AND BODY. YOU CAN HEAL YOUR LIFE.

- Eat nutritious food to help start healing your brain and body.
- The correct wholesome, nutritional vitamins or supplements will help too.
- Read scriptures to bring life to your soul.
- Pray always.
- Walking for exercise, balances the body. Depending on where you live, you may want to walk with a friend. There is more safety in numbers. Walking in nature is healing, as well.
- You are precious. You are loved. You can do anything positive toward your health that you set your mind to do. Don't worry about what other people may or may not think about your efforts. There isn't anyone who has the right to judge your efforts or your soul. Do you understand, no one can judge you? Only God is your judge.
- What you think about yourself is what counts. What God thinks of you is what counts. GOD LOVES YOU.
- If a professional, medical detox facility or treatment facility is not available, and you are helping someone who is withdrawing from drugs or alcohol; learn all you can about appropriate actions that need to be taken. Call a clinic or hospital for advice, if you need advice. Withdrawing from certain substances, if not done correctly, can be fatal. An example of this is withdrawing from a severe alcohol addiction or large amounts of alcohol in a person's body. During this detox period, alcohol consumption must be slowly decreased in appropriate amounts. The amounts are different for each person. Therefore, detoxing is serious and must be done with knowledge, care, and good judgment.
- Sometimes a person who is under the influence of drugs or alcohol, or who is withdrawing from drugs or alcohol may exhibit actions that are undesirable, and/or un-predictable. This is due to the effects of drugs or alcohol. Please be careful, and always use caution. Use good judgment in all that you do or don't do. Pray always for guidance from the Holy Spirit.

Chapter 11

Prayer, Accepting the Healing Power of Jesus Christ

From one human being to another, God's love is flowing through me to you right now. I am praying for you. During times throughout my life, I will continue to pray and fast for you. People who really care are praying for your success. Always know this.

Victory Scriptures

For we do not wrestle against flesh and blood, but against principalities, against powers, against the rulers of the darkness of this age, against spiritual hosts of wickedness in the heavenly places. Therefore, take up the whole armor of God, that you may be able to withstand in the evil day, and having done all, to stand. Ephesians 6:12-13

Let us touch and agree to ask right now, "Dear God, in the name of your Son, Jesus Christ to please forgive my sins. I have accepted you in my life and my being. I thank you for your sacrifice at the cross, and know my sins are forgiven. Keep me free from anything that may harm my life. Keep me safe, away from snares or temptations of the adversary. Show your might through me dear Lord. Your power, working through me to make the right choices. The choices for my life, according to your Will. I accept the blood of Christ in my life and being. In my human weakness, I know I have strength in you. Thank you for your love and for salvation. In Jesus name, I pray. Amen."

Put on the whole armor of God, that ye may be able to stand against the wiles of the devil. Ephesians 6:11

Therefore, take up the whole armor of God, that you may be able to withstand in the evil day, and having done all, to stand.

Stand therefore, having girded your waist with truth, having put on the breastplate of righteousness, and having shod your feet with the preparation of the gospel of peace; above all, taking the shield of faith with which, you will be able to quench all the fiery darts of the wicked one. And take the helmet of salvation, and the sword of the Spirit, which is the word of God; praying always with all prayer and supplication in the Spirit, being watchful to this end with all perseverance and supplication for all the saints – and for me, that utterance may be given me, that I may open my mouth boldly to make known the mystery of the gospel, for which I am an ambassador in chains; that in it I may speak boldly, as I ought to speak. Ephesians 6:13-20

Through Christ's sufferings, and by his blood, we are healed and already have victory. Know this, and put on the full armor of God. Accept His healing.

Inasmuch then as the children have partaken of flesh and blood, He Himself likewise shared in the same, that through death He might destroy him who had the power of death, that is, the devil, and release those who through fear of death were all their lifetime subject to bondage. Hebrews 2:14-15

But you, brethren are not in darkness, so that this Day should overtake you as a thief. You are all sons of light and sons of the day. We are not of the night nor of darkness. Therefore, let us not sleep, as others do, but let us watch and be sober. 1 Thessalonians 5:4-6

Then they cried out to the Lord in their trouble, And He saved them out of their distresses. He sent his word and healed them; and delivered them from their destructions. Psalm 107:19-20

"Come to me, all you who are weary and burdened, and I will give you rest. Take my yoke upon you and learn from me, for I am gentle and humble in heart, and you will find rest for your souls. For my yoke is easy and my burden is light." Mathew 11:28-30 NIV

Heal me, Lord, and I will be healed; save me and I will be saved, for you are the one I praise. Jeremiah 17:14 NIV

He said to her, "Daughter, your faith has healed you. Go in peace and be freed from your suffering." Mark 5:34 NIV

And the prayer of faith will save the sick, and the Lord will raise him up. And if he has committed sins, he will be forgiven. Confess your trespasses to one another and pray for one another, that you may be healed. The effective, fervent prayer of a righteous man avails much. James 5:15-16

Be kind and compassionate to one another, forgiving each other, just as in Christ God forgave you. Ephesians 4:32 NIV

Therefore, as God's chosen people, holy and dearly loved, clothe yourselves with compassion, kindness, humility, gentleness and patience. Colossians 3:12 NIV

And for this reason, He is the Mediator of the new covenant, by means of death, for the redemption of the transgressions under the first covenant, that those who are called may receive the promise of the eternal inheritance. Hebrews 9:15

And having been perfected, He became the author of eternal salvation to all who obey Him. Hebrews 5:9

But You, O Lord, are a shield for me, My glory, and the One who lifts up my head. Psalm 3:3

For with You is the fountain of life; In Your light we see light. Psalm 36:9

Chapter 12

Be Wise in Dealing with People

Grace to you and peace from God our Father and the Lord Jesus Christ. Blessed be the God and Father of our Lord Jesus Christ, the Father of mercies and God of all comfort, who comforts us in all our tribulation, that we may be able to comfort those who are in any trouble, with the comfort with which we ourselves are comforted by God. For as the sufferings of Christ abound in us, so our consolation also abounds through Christ. 2 Corinthians 1:2-5

If you feel as though you may need someone to talk to, reach out to people who really care about you. People who are non-judgmental. People who you can trust.

And let us consider one another in order to stir up love and good works, not forsaking the assembling of ourselves together, as is the manner of some, but exhorting one another, and so much the more as you see the Day approaching. Hebrews 10:24-25

In your everyday life, keep in mind, not all people who claim to be Christian are real followers of Christ. In this day and age, there is so much hypocrisy you need to be careful. There are people who will take advantage of someone in distress. In later years, in a distressing situation, I made a mistake in reaching out to someone who claimed to be Christian, but was not. She acted and said all the right things. Then took advantage of a situation. This happens to people sometimes. Be wise in your dealings with people.

Behold, I send you out as sheep in the midst of wolves. Therefore, be wise as serpents and harmless as doves. Mathew 10:16

When You Need to Talk

You may want to share your feelings, or just talk about things with trustworthy friends. Your friends want you to reach out to them. They care about you. You are important to them. Sometimes, you may feel as though you don't want to bother your friends, by telling them how much you are hurting. Not reaching out, is a big mistake. You are not a bother. Your real friends want you to reach out to them. They treasure your friendship more than you know.

If you do not have this type of friendship or if you have an urgent need to talk in a crisis or need help, you can call the suicide hot line at 800-273-8255. Please call them. They are here to help. Please reach out to them. People care.
Call 800-273-8255

Suicide Hotline

Please call.

We all face challenges at one time or another. There may be times when you are not able to be in contact with anyone at all. During these times, you must be there for yourself. Many times, each of us must be there for ourselves. Trust yourself, as you would a true best friend. Comfort yourself as a true best friend would comfort you. Stand up for yourself as a real friend would stand up for you. Have fun with yourself as you would have fun with a friend.

When I was a teenager, I read a book entitled "How to be Your Own Best Friend," by Mildred Newman and Bernard Berkowitz. The message of being your own best friend stuck with me.

Be your own best friend.

There are other resources you may want to use to help you through difficult times.

Support Groups

You may want to join a bereavement support group. Each group is coordinated differently. In these groups you may get assistance with understanding the grief process and assistance with problem solving and managing emotional stress. You may obtain literature or information regarding community resources in your area. Being in the company of other people who are going through some of the things you are going through may give you a feeling of connectedness. Even if some meetings are on internet forums such as zoom. It's healthy for people to give and receive support from each other. Some people enjoy attending these groups.

Mental Health Counseling

Sometimes, some people find counselling as a good resource. Some educated, intuitive, caring professionals in the mental health field may be a resource for you. There are psychiatrists, psychologists, therapists, counselors, or grief counselors who you may want to talk to. Most of these services cost money or take medical insurance. You may or may not have to wait for an appointment. If you do not have medical insurance and are unable to afford counselling. There may be resources in your area providing these services for reduced rates.

Finding a good, knowledgeable, intuitive counselor you can trust, may take time. If this is what you need or want, don't give up. Don't ever give up on anything in life. A good counselor who you can trust, can help give insight, and get you through challenging times in your life.

Do not be anxious about anything, but in every situation, by prayer and petition, with thanksgiving, present your requests to God. And the peace of God, which transcends all understanding, will guard your hearts and your minds in Christ Jesus. Philippians 4:6-7 NIV

Sometimes colleges or universities have students majoring in psychology who provide counseling at the university, at reduced rates or for free for the community. Perhaps there may be organizations in your area who have counselling or peer support volunteers. Your church may have members who help with counselling, as well. Remember, in an emergency; you can go to a hospital emergency department.

Sharing Grief

You may also talk with your family members. You will have to use good judgment if your loved one was special in their lives too. Because, they are grieving, as well. Family members who love you, care about what you are going through. You will know whether talking about your feelings together will be healing for both of you. For some families, sharing parts of this grieving journey is healing. May peace be with all of you.

You Can Talk to God (Your Heavenly Father)

Cast your burden on the Lord, And He shall sustain you; He shall never permit the righteous to be moved. Psalm 55:22

Now may the God of hope fill you with all joy and peace in believing, that you may abound in hope by the power of the Holy Spirit. Romans 15:13

Chapter 13

Time Heals Wounds

My wounds were so deep, I didn't think time would heal them.

With the passage of time, a long period of time, my pain slowly decreased.

Healing started to happen. Time must have a way of healing, separate from what we do, in trying to heal ourselves. I realized this when I could finally speak of what happened without crying. When I speak of my husband now, I can smile or laugh during the conversation. When I speak of my mom and dad now, it's with joy of their memory. With gratitude of their love.

When I speak of friends who have passed, I can share the grandness of their lives, instead of the sadness of their passing.

Over the years, in speaking with people in grief, or on their healing journey. I learned people do indeed grieve differently. For example, some people choose to go back to work right away, putting all their time into their jobs or careers. While others, if given the choice, choose not to work for a period of time. For some people, it was necessary for them to stay busy. For others, it was necessary to be still and have more quiet moments. You will make the right choice for you, and your family.

Stages of Grief

There are stages of grief that are different for each person. You may
or may not experience these stages, or additional stages. You may
want to use them as a point of reference. Or continue to study about
stages of grief in more detail, if it is helpful for your healing. Over the
years, several authors have written about stages of grief.
Dr. Elisabeth Kubler-Ross is a psychiatrist and author who wrote
extensively about grief, and healing.

In 1969, the five stages of grief according to Swiss-American
psychiatrist Elisabeth Kubler-Ross are denial, anger, bargaining,
depression, and acceptance. Dr. Kubler-Ross's work was highly
respected.

Stages of grief are different for each person. For example, a person
could go through all of the stages, just to end up back at the first
stage again.

Or the stages may move around. There are additional stages as well.

Grief does not have a set pattern. Grief is personal and unpredictable.
There aren't any easy answers. If you can relate to these five stages,
you may be able to use it as a tool to help with understanding some
of your feelings. Only you know what you are experiencing. Only you
know what you must do for healing.

The First Year

After the death of a loved one, the first year of grieving is the most difficult for most people. It will be the first holidays you will experience without your loved one's physical presence. Special times like birthdays, Valentine's Day, Thanksgiving, and Christmas may evoke unexpected feelings or reactions. It may help to take measures in safeguarding your well-being by planning in advance what you will do on a special occasion or to celebrate each holiday. Whatever you decide to do. Your loved ones want you to enjoy the holidays in peace and comfort. They want you to celebrate their life, by respecting and celebrating yours.

A Best Friend's Healing Journey

Janet, one of my best friend's husband passed away years before my husband did. When her husband passed away. She missed him very much. I saw extreme sadness in her eyes. In her eyes I also saw strength and peace. As though the Holy Spirit was working through her.

In mourning, Janet came to work calm and composed, while filling out her requests for bereavement leave. Later, she took a few years off to spend quality time with her young daughter. Then she went back to work for years, before successfully retiring.

Janet continued living in the home she and her husband shared. She left his clothes hanging in the closets just as he left them. She'd speak of him in such a special way, a person felt warm inside, listening to her. She kept her husband's memory alive. She was grateful for him and the life they shared together. While grieving, she cherished her life. She remained the strength of her family. With loving grace, and a compassionate, generous heart she cared for her family members, and friends.

Janet gave so much of herself to people. She would go into the hospitals or nursing homes to cut and style patient's hair for them. Patients who were not able to leave the hospital. She had been a licensed cosmetologist earlier in her life. And although she had other careers, she kept her license current. She was happy about this – feeling the rewards of watching people enjoy a new haircut. Often, she'd stay with the patient, conversing and laughing with them.

Janet enjoyed knitting. She knitted hats and gloves to donate to children in the community. She knitted blankets for her friends, and blankets to donate to charity. I still treasure the nice blanket with various deep shades of pink she gave me.

I could tell her anything in trust. She'd listen intently, talked with me, never judging, always uplifting. She was like a sister to me, an aunt to my children. Janet was always there for me. There for everyone who needed and loved her. I only hope my life touched hers as much as her life touched mine. We all still miss her.

She is with her loving husband again.

When Janet's husband died, her time of living without his physical presence seemed long. She missed him very much – his touch – his laughter.

Before she expected. Before all of us expected. The time came for her to be with her husband again. Janet is with our Lord and Savior, in pure joy.

March 19, 1951 – March 2, 2015

And I give them eternal life, and they shall never perish, neither shall anyone snatch them out of my hand. John 10:28

Chapter 14

When Grief is Finished?

Odyssey Health Care Hospice was very helpful to our family during my dad's final days of mortal life. They brought medical equipment and medication to dad's home. And took time explaining everything to us in a kind, compassionate manner.

I really appreciate the nurse who came to our home. Their sincere care and follow up is appreciated.

After dad's funeral, Odyssey Health Care staff kept in touch with us by sending letters and good information. After a year or so, they sent me this letter with the heading "When Grief is Finished." I'm sharing it with you on the next page.

Everlasting Life Scriptures

Now, may the God of hope fill you with all joy and peace in believing, that you may abound in hope by the power of the Holy Spirit. Romans 15:13

Most assuredly, I say to you, he who hears My word and believes in Him who sent Me has everlasting life, and shall not come into judgment, but has passed from death into life. Most assuredly, I say to you, the hour is coming, and now is when the dead will hear the voice of the Son of God; and those who hear will live. For as the Father has life in Himself, so He has granted the Son to have life in Himself, and has given Him authority to execute judgment also, because He is the Son of Man. Do not marvel at this; for the hour is coming in which all who are in the graves will hear His voice and come forth - those who have done good, to the resurrection of life, and those who have done evil, to the resurrection of condemnation. John 5:24-29

Odyssey HealthCare

When is Grief Finished?
By Jim Metzler and Craig Greer, Chaplains

In one sense, there is no finish line to grief. When a loved one dies, we will always miss the relationship we had with that person. Sometimes we will re-experience the pain of that loss as we go through annual celebrations such as birthdays, holidays and anniversaries.

Nonetheless we are called back into the land of the living and our daily responsibilities. Reinvesting in life and significant relationships is the key to getting through our grief. Realizing life is forever changed by the death of a loved one, gives us permission to begin building a new life with their memory in our hearts.

Building upon our experiences of the past can lead us to a new future. While the death of our loved one was not our choice, how we respond to that loss is a choice we must make. To move forward we must settle or be at peace with unresolved issues, accept the reality that our life has changed, allow ourselves to let go of guilt and resentment regarding the death of our loved one and recommit to our lives.

How do you know you are moving on? The following signs of healing are adapted from Costa's *Handbook for the Bereaved.*

- You can talk about your loved one without getting a lump in your throat
- You can enjoy memories and even look at pictures without becoming depressed
- You can share your feelings with someone and not be overwhelmed
- You feel more in control of your emotions
- Self-esteem returns and you take pride in yourself
- Ability to focus on others and get involved in other activities
- Life holds new meaning and purpose
- You begin to plan ahead and think of the future without dread
- You are able to laugh and enjoy life without feeling guilty

Finally, the goal is to move from grief to gratitude.
When we are able to see the gift of having had our loved one in our life,
When we appreciate the good and the difficult experiences that were a part of that relationship,
When we can forgive and accept forgiveness for past mistakes,
When we understand the relationship is a part of the fabric of our life,
When we recognize that every moment we spent with that person was a gift
Then we can be grateful for the moments we shared with that person in our life.

2000 SouthBridge Parkway Suite 150 • Birmingham, AL 35209
Phone: (205) 870-4340 • Toll Free: (888) 287-9259 • Fax: (205) 870-9928

Chapter 15

Gratitude and Appreciation

Blessed be the God and Father of our Lord Jesus Christ, the Father of mercies and God of all comfort, who comforts us in all our tribulation, that we may be able to comfort those who are in any trouble, with the comfort with which we ourselves are comforted.

Comfort may sometimes be relevant depending on a person's circumstances. Receiving a genuine smile or greeting from a passing stranger. Or receiving a sincere, kind word from someone at a grocery store might make all the difference in someone's life.

During my time of initial grieving in 2004 and 2005 many caring people reached out to my family.

A woman at Greater Friendship Baptist Church in Anchorage, answered the phone one day, when I was too weak to pray for myself. She prayed for me. Her impactful intercessory prayer lifted me to a higher place. Thank you, my Sister in Christ.

An associate in the Shaklee business, Ms. Barbara Price stopped by our home, just to say hello and bring us a gallon of ice-cream. She told me she had been out grocery shopping; running errands, and thought about us. How nice of her to take the time to stop what she was doing in the middle of her errands to bring us ice-cream. Just knowing we were thought of, brought cheer to my day. Thank you again, Barbara.

A woman, representing the Veterans of Foreign Wars (VFW) on Oklahoma street came to our home. She gave us a beautiful card. She visited with me, telling me about many wonderful words and acts my husband said or did while he visited the VFW. She told me how he really made a good impression on them, and that they would miss him very much.

Thank you again Ms. Rose and the women of the VFW.

A woman from the Municipal Solid Waste Services, where my husband worked, came to our home. Each time she came to visit, we felt her sincere warmth, kindness, and comfort. One day she came to our home just to give me a beautiful card, signed by Municipality of Anchorage Employees.

I could tell she empathized with our pain. She also surprised me with a generous, gift from caring employees who worked for the Municipality. Thank you again.

Years later, while I was vacationing in Hawaii, I made this lei of flowers with the thought of giving the lei to special people in my life. In this book I present this Honorary Lei to Mrs. Florence (Robert) Henderson who transitioned to be with our Lord and Savior on October 16th, 2019 in Anchorage, Alaska.

Letters

Letter to Mrs. Florence Henderson:

I continue to appreciate your example of grace, courage, and strength.

One day in 2004 when I was grieving, you called me to see how I was doing. You suggested for me to:

- get up every morning
- take a shower
- wear something pretty that makes me feel good
- put on make-up or fix my hair in a way that makes me feel good
- and greet the day with thankfulness.

I remember telling you that I could not do that because my life energy was gone – my life energy died with my husband.

You patiently understood. You prayed for me. You told me I would one day feel life again. You continued to be one of the greatest mentors in my life. Since then, I have shared your advice with many people who were and are grieving. Some of these people were able to do what you said, and told me your advice helped them. Thank You.

Thank You Pastor Ivery L. Henderson for your inspirational, uplifting sermons. I know for a fact the Holy Spirit was speaking through you many times. Thank you for your example of perseverance and courage. Thank you for your kind words of encouragement regarding motherhood. You often gave me that extra boost of confidence in my role as a mother in Christ Jesus. Thank you for praying for me and my family. I have much respect for you. With the love of Christ, I thank you.

Thank you to one of my children's closest, childhood friends, a young man who I consider my son, Mr. Wah'Fe L. Granger of Anchorage, Alaska and Chester, Pennsylvania. September 17, 1992 – November 21, 2020

Letter to Wah'Fe:

Wah'Fe, the many ways in which you gave us joy will take another book. When Big Rich passed away, you were there for me. Sometimes you would come to our home on your way to or from football practice, just to cheer me up. I remember one day when I was sitting on my living room floor, very sad, missing Big Rich, you showed up. You compassionately said with your sweet, tender voice.

"C'mon Ms. Brenda, you can't just sit around sad all day. Snap out of it."

You helped me up off the floor. You told a joke and made me laugh. Thank you for the laughter.

Memories of you playing in our yard, rapping music, dancing in our home; having fun with our family will stay with us forever.

I remember the day you, your mother, my son and I went to the Alaska Native Heritage Center. We really enjoyed watching the Native cultural dances and joining in the many activities there. We all had so much fun! I cherish the pictures of all of us.

I remember when you were either 9, 10, or 11 years old.

Do you remember the day I took you along with 3 other boys to the Fort Richardson gym-swimming pool to go swimming? Do you remember what you forgot to tell me? We can smile and laugh about the swimming pool experience again, when we see each other again.

While you were growing up, I really enjoyed watching you run and win track meets. I really enjoyed watching you play football. Congratulations again on the many championships you earned.

You always had a deep heart-felt love for your family and true friends. I am proud of you for overcoming challenges and being true to yourself. You grew up to be a strong young man. As a young man, you thought of us, your family in Alaska, often. You sent your thoughts and well wishes to all of us. I miss you very much, son.

We love you, Wah'Fe. Thank you for blessing our lives.

Love always and forever,

Your Alaska Mom

For God so loved the world that He gave His only begotten Son, that whoever believes in Him should not perish but have everlasting life. John 3:16

And we know that the Son of God has come and has given us an understanding, that we may know Him who is true; and we are in Him who is true, in His Son Jesus Christ. This is the true God and eternal life. John 5:20

Special Thanks

Special thanks to:

- Mr. George R. Post
- Mrs. Lusiana Hansen
- Ms. Angela Grant
- Ms. Marcia L. Harrison

Looking unto Jesus, the author and finisher of our faith, who for the joy that was set before Him endured the cross, despising the shame, and has sat down at the right hand of the throne of God.
Hebrews 12:2

Gratitude and Appreciation from 2004

My children and I wanted very much to thank each of you in 2004, for your kindness and generosity. Some of you did not know us personally. You reached out to us. Your kindness meant the world to us. Thank you. Thank you to God, my Heavenly Father. Thank you to our family, relatives and friends. Thank you to my cousin Arthur, Brina and family. Thank you to Mrs. Louise Jackson. Thank you to Mrs. Mary Crockett Lipsey. Thank you to Ms. Julia Crockett. Thank you to the United States Army Honor Guard, at Fort Rucker, Alabama. Thank you to Dr. Scott Kelly. Thank you to Dr. Kristopher Wood. Thank you to the Alabama medical staff who cared for my dad. Thank you to the United Airlines representative who helped us at the Alabama airport. Thank you to the representative who saw us safely to our hotel. Thank you to the paramedics at the airport in Alabama. Thank you to the employees of the Municipality of Anchorage Solid Waste Services, Alaska. Thank you to Inlet Petroleum Company. Thank you to VFW (Oklahoma St.) Women's Auxiliary. Thank you to the United States Army Honor Guard at Fort Richardson, Alaska. Thank you to Bishop, Dr. Charles R. Hawkins (Pastor), Mrs. Marie Hawkins, and the True Vine Ministries Family. Thank you to Mr. Samuel John Walker Sr. & Mrs. Blondell (Hattie B.) Walker. Thank you to Pastor Ivery Henderson, True Man of God, & Mrs. Florence Henderson, True Woman of God and Prayer Warrior. Thank you to the staff at Susitna Elementary School. Special thanks to Ms. Dolores Padilla-Kairaiuak, an exemplary, caring teacher. Thank you to Ms. Barbara Price. Thank you to Shanon, Kristy, Brad & Julie, Mrs. Janet Meade, Ms. Crystal Meade, Mrs. Cheryl Grant Carmack, Mr. David Hansen and Mrs. Lusiana Hansen (Lucy). Thank you to Eliza. Thank you to Beata, Jerzy, Nikki, Mathew, and Mario. Thank you to everyone who sent uplifting cards and letters. Thank you to everyone who kept us in prayer.

Thank you.

Thank you to:
Brother and Sister Richard Taylor,
Reverend and Sister Gordon Branch,
Reverend and Sister Otis Raymond, Brother and Sister A. Geer,
Brother Robin Mitra, Sister Sara, Mr. and Mrs. Mike and Ann Vasakis,
Reverend and Sister Craig and Angela Chenery, Mr. Thomas A.,
Mr. Tim Ridle, Ms. Elizabeth Hughes, E. Williams,
Mr. Brian Vanderwood, Mr. David Otto, Ms. Karen Moore,
Ms. Barbara Stallone, Mr. Gordon, Mr. Monett,
Sister Brenda Johnson-Dewitt, Professor Rosanne Pagano,
Ms. Patty Kilson, Ms. Cheryl Chamberlin, Mr. Anderson Vickers,
Mr. Greg Joubert, Mrs. Bernadette Queen & Family,
The Juarez Family – Susan, Danny, & Mindy Juarez,
Ms. Angie Lindberg,
Ms. Dolores Padilla-Kairaiuak, Mr. Cody Kairaiuak, Ms. LaWanda
Queen and Da'Shon, Mr. J.D. Elray, Mr. J. Mowery,
Ms. Theresa Norman,
Ms. Gena Barragan,
Ms. Deneen Nichols, Ms. Estella Manley, Ms. Daphane Mathis,
Mr. Jeffrey Clay, and Ms. Rene Rouzan.

THANK YOU.

Vanderwood, Brian G.

From:	MOA Bulletin Board
Sent:	Monday, June 14, 2004 3:27 PM
To:	!!ALL(postmaster only); !AWWUALL; !APD All Personnel
Subject:	To all Municipal employees:

To all Municipal employees:

It is with deep regret that I inform you that a fellow employee, Richard Genaro, passed away last Thursday evening. Richard was a Solid Waste Sideload operator and leaves behind his wife, Brenda, and three children. Richard will be sorely missed by his family, friends, co-workers and customers. Our deepest condolences go out to all of these people.

Anyone wishing to donate leave to help ease the financial burden on his family may do so through their payroll clerks. We will keep you apprised of services arrangements as soon as we receive the information.

Thank you.

Mayor Begich

Do not reply to this message. Mail to "MOA Bulletin Board" is not monitored.

To Brenda and Family
our thoughts and prayers go out to each of you

Alan Mundt	Mia Nistler
Glenn Byerly	Mike Blair
Brad Bezona	Patricia Kilson
Bryan Protzman	Paul Goodwin
Charles Dorius	Penyon Dade
Cheryl Chamberlin	Ralph Butler
Chuck Magsambol	Raymond Leblanc
David Gunn	Rhonda Littrell
Deatra Scott	Richard Rhyner
Dee Maly	Rick Nissen
Elizabeth Hughes	Robert Steffey
Fred Blagg	Shannon Foland
Gary Gordon	Sondra Scobee
Jack McAllister	Steve Cooper
James Brown	Susan Williams
Jeffrey Myers	Terry Kelly
Jennifer Dearinger	Todd Winter
Joseph Kelly	Vince Lamb
Kelli Ayers	Will Askren
Leroy Branch	William Hixenbaugh
Mari Johnston	

THANK YOU.

Conclusion

The Beatitudes

And seeing the multitudes, He went up on a mountain, and when He was seated His disciples came to Him. Then He opened His mouth and taught them, saying:

"Blessed are the poor in spirit, For theirs is the kingdom of heaven,

Blessed are those who mourn, For they shall be comforted.

Blessed are the meek, For they shall inherit the earth.

Blessed are those who hunger and thirst for righteousness, For they shall be filled.

Blessed are the merciful, For they shall obtain mercy.

Blessed are the pure in heart, For they shall see God.

Blessed are the peacemakers, For they shall be called sons of God.

Blessed are those who are persecuted for righteousness' sake, For theirs is the kingdom of Heaven. Mathew 5:3-10

And I am sure of this, that he who began a good work in you will bring it to completion at the day of Jesus Christ. Philippians 1:6 ESV

NOTES FOR YOUR JOURNEY

JOURNEY NOTES

JOURNEY NOTES

JOURNEY NOTES

JOURNEY NOTES

JOURNEY NOTES

JOURNEY NOTES

JOURNEY NOTES

JOURNEY NOTES

JOURNEY NOTES

JOURNEY NOTES

JOURNEY NOTES

JOURNEY NOTES

JOURNEY NOTES

JOURNEY NOTES

JOURNEY NOTES

JOURNEY NOTES

JOURNEY NOTES

JOURNEY NOTES

JOURNEY NOTES

JOURNEY NOTES

JOURNEY NOTES

JOURNEY NOTES

JOURNEY NOTES

JOURNEY NOTES

JOURNEY NOTES

About the Author

The author was born in Clark Air Force Base, Philippines. Her father served in the United States Army. Her mother was a school teacher. After her mother married her father, she left a rewarding teaching career, to be a dedicated wife and mother. Their family traveled together during her father's military service. Traits of generosity, compassion, kindness, hard-work, and faith were traits the author's parents exemplified in her life.

The author wanted to reach out to you during your times of grief, with a deep desire for your healing, and success. The author's love of humanity, gifts of the Holy Spirit, and intuitive nature has been appreciated by countless people whom she has helped, in many aspects, during difficult times. She is now a CEO in an exemplary organization whose focus is to improve the lives of people that have challenges regarding mental health, addiction, and life skills. She enjoys gardening, nature, exercise, and writing.

Author Contact Information:

WriteBrenda@Everlasting Life Reminder.com

Website: EverlastingLifeReminder.com

www.ingramcontent.com/pod-product-compliance
Lightning Source LLC
Chambersburg PA
CBHW072158090426
42740CB00012B/2309